# Fascinating People
*and*
# Astounding Events
*from the*
# History of the
# Western World

# Fascinating People
## *and*
# Astounding Events
## *from the*
# History of the
# Western World

RONALD D. SMITH

**ABC-CLIO**

Santa Barbara, California
Oxford, England

**Library of Congress Cataloging-in-Publication Data**
Smith, Ronald D., 1935–
    Fascinating people and astounding events from the history of the
Western World / Ronald D. Smith.
      p. cm.
    Includes bibliographical references.
    1. World history—Miscellanea.  I. Title.
    D21.3.S55    1989    909—dc20    89-17964

ISBN 0-87436-544-9 (alk. paper)

96 95 94 93 92        10 9 8 7 6 5 4 3 2

ABC-CLIO, Inc.
130 Cremona Drive, P.O. Box 1911
Santa Barbara, California 93116-1911

Clio Press Ltd.
55 St. Thomas' Street
Oxford, OX1 1JG, England

This book is Smyth-sewn and printed on acid-free paper ∞
Manufactured in the United States of America

# Contents

# Chapter III: Renaissance and Reformation Era, 65

# Chapter IV: The Seventeenth Century, 91

# Chapter VII: The Twentieth Century, 151

# Preface

This volume of anecdotes and short essays, pertaining to Western civilization from ancient times to the mid-twentieth century, is a resource for social studies teachers and students. It arms the teacher with interesting and relevant materials that the student is not likely to meet in standard reading, thereby enlivening class presentations. It also provides to the student an unusual research resource. The chapters are arranged in chronological sequence, with selections that include the ancient world and the medieval world, and a twentieth-century collection that concludes with the end of World War II and the opening of the cold war era. Within chapters, anecdotes are grouped by time and place, each with a descriptive heading. A subject index makes it easy to locate selections on particular persons or events.

The topics of these selections represent the experience of this author over nearly 30 years of teaching European history. All of the anecdotes have proven to be effective teaching aids. The collection includes descriptions of ironic incidents, cases of extreme behavior that was a direct result of historical developments, biographical data that helps to explain historical events, and, in some cases, refutation of long-standing misconceptions. A modest and general bibliography has been included to reveal the kinds of sources employed and to encourage further study.

# Suggestions for Teachers

The primary purpose of these anecdotes is to provide teachers with tools to whet students' historical appetites. Thus, several suggestions are provided as to how these selections might be used most effectively. These small bits of information may be used as bait to lead a student to appreciate and understand a significant body of general knowledge. The anecdotes that follow discuss the rise of monasticism, the optimism and self-assurance of statesmen whose thinking was formed during the Enlightenment, and a historical fact about the life of Jesus Christ. All can be used independently, but also can serve to embellish and portray the foundations for a greater understanding of historical periods or events.

## The Rise of Monasticism

Students are not likely to throw themselves into reading about the Middle Ages if led only by the general term "monasticism"; a brief story may tease their interest. The teacher might tell the class about an early and extreme example of ascetic practices, namely, the career of Saint Simeon Stylites (390?–459). After some preliminary severities, such as spending a summer as a rooted vegetable in a garden and wearing a spiked girdle, he built himself a column near Antioch on which he lived for 30 years. The circumference of the top of the column measured little more than three feet and had a railing that kept the saint from falling while he slept. Disciples brought food and water for his meager diet. He bound himself to the pillar with rope, which in time became embedded in his flesh and caused infection. His flesh putrefied around the rope and teemed with maggots. Simeon Stylites picked up the worms that fell from his sores and replaced them, saying, "Eat what God has given you." From his perch, the saint preached, shamed moneylenders, and converted barbarians.

Such a story should certainly leave students curious about why someone would behave as Saint Simeon Stylites did. The ground is thus prepared for the instructor to explain that some people did not like the early changes in the Christian Church, which resulted from growth and expanded wealth and organization. Such people tried to become closer to God by engaging in behaviors that would push pleasure or comfort from their minds because they believed that pleasure drew them away from God. Comparisons could be drawn among the Benedictines of the sixth century; the monks of the Carolingian Renaissance; the early missionaries; various orders such as the Cistercians, Dominicans, and Franciscans; and finally the Jesuits of the sixteenth century.

## The Enlightenment

In a unit on the Age of Reason (rationalism) and the Enlightenment, the teacher must supply the cultural and intellectual links that led to the widely expressed belief that man, by his own ability to reason, could construct society and governmental institutions for the benefit of all. An understanding of this view is crucial to the study of the period that led to the American and French revolutions. One technique to help students reach this understanding is merely to ask whether they believe that the soldiers of the Persian king Xerxes (486–465 B.C.) were once children. All will say that they do. Then ask whether students believe they could secure concrete proof that these soldiers were once children; there will likely be no response. Next, ask whether they are still willing to believe that the soldiers were once children; most or all of the students will say that they do believe this even though there is no documentary proof. Reason, based on experience, tells them that the soldiers of King Xerxes were once children.

Having made this point, the teacher can quote Thomas Jefferson's words from the Declaration of Independence: "We hold these truths to be self evident, that all men were created equal, and were endowed by their creator with certain inalienable rights." Jefferson could not prove that claim with irrefutable or demonstrable evidence. It is significant that neither he nor his comrades saw any need to do so, because this explains the political outlook of the late eighteenth century, which created a receptive atmosphere for pamphlets such as Thomas Paine's *Common Sense,* the Abbé Sieyès's "What Is the Third Estate?" and the Declaration of the Rights of Man, which appeared during the early years of the French Revolution.

## Jesus and Wine

Did Jesus drink wine? Both the asking and the answering of this question serve a serious educational purpose. Of course, the Scriptures indicate that Jesus did drink wine, in the episodes of the changing of water into wine and of the Last Supper. But asking this question also provides opportunities to discuss other aspects of life in the Near East during the reign of Caesar Augustus (31 B.C.–A.D. 14). For example, in the ancient world there were no food companies like Heinz or Del Monte that canned or froze the juice of grapes. Yet there was an urgent need to preserve both the nutritional (iron) and caloric properties of grapes, a crop blessed by the particular terrain and climate of the Near East. In the form of wine, grapes could be preserved and retained in heavy earthenware containers, thus meeting a crucial need for humans and also rendering the soil, vines, and fruit more valuable to the economy. This information brings a further dimension to the story of Jesus changing the water into wine, since wine's nutritional value was probably one of the main reasons that it was preferred over water. All of this discussion might lead students to ask why some Christian churches employ wine for Holy Communion and others do not; the teacher could furnish additional relevant information or suggest that the question be considered when the era of the Protestant Reformation and, more specifically, the development of Puritanism and pietism are studied. The teacher could also use this story to illustrate the economic significance of a crop such as grapes to such modern European nations as Italy, France, Germany, Greece, Spain, and Portugal.

Each of the following chapters includes a short overview that the teacher should read prior to examining the Questions for Discussion. After reading the selections the teacher should be able to answer the questions and relate each selection's significance in the larger picture of historical events that shaped the course of European development.

# CHAPTER I

# The Ancient World

Diverse people such as Sumerians, Medes, Lydians, Hittites, Egyptians, Assyrians, Babylonians, and Persians all left their cultural stamp on the history of the Near East. The Greeks were heirs to the rich contributions of their predecessors, a reality reflected in their law codes, literature, coinage, commerce, and forms of government. While defeat of the Persian armies afforded security from the non-Greek peoples of the East, the golden years of Greece lasted less than a century and ended with two leagues of Greek city-states locked in civil war. Though Sparta eventually gained a military victory over Athens and her allies, the weakened pillars of Greek society made it possible for the peninsula to be overrun by Macedonian forces and integrated into Alexander's empire and, later, into the Roman Empire. The five-century Roman rise to Mediterranean dominance began but one year before Athens' golden age. By the time of Jesus Christ, the Roman republic on the Tiber had expanded through a combination of war and diplomacy to include areas as far removed as old Babylonia and southern England. A full two centuries before the commencement of Rome's decline the world witnessed the birth of Christianity, a faith concerned with the spiritual rather than the physical world. This faith presided at the Roman Empire's funeral and became the chief heir of Roman institutions. Christianity played a central role both in the closing chapter of the Roman story and in the opening chapter of the medieval story.

## Questions for Discussion

- Hundreds of millions of dollars are spent on modern Olympic competition. How important were such competitions to the Greeks? Did the Romans demonstrate a great appreciation for spectator sports? What were the differences between the Greek and the Roman games?

- Did Greek culture reach a level of sophistication that included enjoyment of the theater, the use of beauty aids, and themes of romantic love?

- How did Socrates demonstrate his shrewdness?

- In addition to a simple translation of the term *pax Romana,* what other aspects might be included in its definition to provide a more complete understanding?

- How did the Roman Emperor Vespasian respond to his son's criticism of heavy taxation?

- What were some of the characteristics of the Roman emperors Caligula and Nero, who were condemned by Roman historians and gossips?

- Did Pontius Pilate view Jesus as a serious threat to his administration? Why was Jesus crucified? Was crucifixion a punishment that had a specific judicial purpose?

- Did the Roman historian Tacitus see some of the same traits that had helped to build Rome in the virility and adventurous character of the Teutonic tribesmen from beyond the empire's northern frontiers?

- What Christian definition of sin is to be learned from Saint Augustine's confession to stealing pears?

- Why was purple the most valuable color for ancient and medieval cloth? Would its value explain why purple became the official color of royalty and other rulers?

# EARLY NEAR EAST

## *The Horse: A Step in Political Evolution*

During the middle part of the second millennium B.C. there occurred what might properly be termed a technological breakthrough in warfare—the emergence of the horse. Prior to this time the ox and the ass had served the primary functions of pulling and transporting. Anthropologists believe the horse arrived in the Middle East as a result of incursions by Indo-European peoples from the plains to the north. This animal that had the combined abilities of speed and strength stimulated the use of cavalry and, more particularly, the use of chariots. The introduction of the stirrup during the Middle Ages further enhanced the significance of the horse and played a role in the development of chivalry. A demand for more metals and other strong, flexible materials was the result, to say nothing of the increased economic investment in or expense of military operations.

## *Rameses II: A Demigod*

Rameses II (1300–1233 B.C.) was the last of the great and flamboyant pharaohs; his reign is of special interest to students of the Near East, and no doubt also to U.S. and European movie buffs who consider one of Yul Brynner's most memorable roles that of the commanding Egyptian ruler in *The Ten Commandments.*

Rameses was no doubt brave and handsome. He launched victorious military campaigns in Nubia, Palestine, and Asia and inherited or completed many of the great structures and artworks that became both contributions to the future and revelations about his long reign. He married 100 wives and had 100 sons along with 50 daughters. The Egyptian religion viewed the pharaoh as a demigod, which helps us understand how this familial legacy created an elite class that practiced ongoing intermarriage and from which future rulers were chosen. After all, gods would not marry mere human beings. This is what provoked one critic to claim that Cleopatra was the result of a dozen generations of incest.

Knowing about this aspect of ancient Egypt also helps us to understand why, when Alexander the Great (d. 323 B.C.) conquered Egypt, he did not limit his role to that of a general, but took on all the deified trappings that went with the office of pharaoh.

Rameses II appears to have been the pharaoh in Genesis 45 who ruled over an empire that included the pastoral lands to the south identified as Goshen. According to the limited account in the Old Testament, we know that Rameses conquered Palestine, and it is likely that many Jews were brought to Egypt as slaves. But documentation of the full details of the later Exodus still eludes us.

## An Eye for an Eye

The great Hammurabi (c. 1704–1662 B.C.), able military and civil ruler of the city-state of Babylon, ultimately gained control over the entire Tigris-Euphrates Valley. His legacy was one of the supreme achievements of humankind up through the seventeenth century—a law code touching civil, criminal, social, and family affairs. If we consider Egypt's Rameses II a contemporary of Moses, then the code of Hammurabi antedates the Hebrew written laws of the Pentateuch by nearly 500 years.

The law code was carved in 3,600 lines on a stone column about 8 feet high. This column was discovered near Susa by French archaeologists in 1901. It was removed to a museum in the West (Paris), just as many other ancient Near Eastern treasures have been.

It is evident from the laws that compose the code that ancient Babylon was a society of three classes, with slaves at the bottom. Hammurabi's code provided "eye for an eye" (the code uses "tooth") retributions in personal tort actions, similar to Mosaic law, and it viewed women as equal to men. The following parts of the code are particularly similar to both Hebrew laws and more modern examples:

1. As in the Old Testament, bearing false witness against another was a serious crime, the penalty being death

2. Agricultural property and animals were sufficiently valuable that negligence causing damage or loss of either was a capital crime

3. A woman who was "a gadabout, thus neglecting her house and humiliating her husband, they shall throw that woman into the water" (the penalty for a woman convicted of adultery in John Calvin's Geneva, c. 1545, was drowning)

4. All torts committed by members of a lower class against members of a higher class carried more serious penalties

The breadth of Hammurabi's code is revealed by its entry number 215, which sets a specific price of ten shekels of silver for successful major surgery.

## Significance of Bread Wheat

If, as most anthropologists believe, one of the greatest steps in human evolution was the shift from nomadic life to village agriculture, then no event was more significant than the appearance of bread wheat some time after 8000 B.C. A genetic accident created a hybrid from a combination of wild wheat and goat grass, a hybrid called emmer that provided a full and enlarged head of seeds that detached easily and greatly expanded the volume for each plant. As Professor Jacob Bronowski claims in his *Ascent of Man*, the combination of water and the new bread wheat made Jericho a city well before the biblical account and probably explains why Joshua led the tribes of Israel to that oasis on their way to the Promised Land.

Once humans were relieved of the continuous wanderings made necessary by sparse-yielding grains, large communities protected by walls began to develop and there was increased productivity in various areas, brought about by such inventions as the plough. The strength and human endurance provided by protein also points to the consumption of meat by early humans as a crucial step in the evolutionary chain.

# HELLENIC AND HELLENISTIC PERIOD

## Greece's Olympic Games

The ancient Panhellenic Games first commenced in the sixth century B.C. and by 476 B.C. were attracting competitors from Greek trading ports as far away as Marseilles and Sinope. If a war was being fought, a one-month truce was proclaimed for the games and festival, and fines were levied upon any Greek city or state in whose territory an athlete en route was molested. Even Philip of Macedonia paid a fine because some of his soldiers robbed an Athenian who was on his way to the games. There was a wide variety of contests but the pentathlon was the most important. The pentathlon included the standing broad jump (with weights in each hand), the discus throw, the javelin throw, a sprint of some 200 yards, and wrestling. One had to win at least three events to win the pentathlon; wrestling was always last among the five, for in this contest a participant might easily be incapacitated.

Wrestling was the most dangerous sport in ancient Olympic competition. The contest was held on a surface that was much the same as modern clay tennis courts—very hard. Athletes wrestled nude, and the rules allowed almost anything. Eyes could be gouged and a participant might grasp any appendage that hung from the body. Serious injury or death usually resulted from one particular maneuver in which competitor A picked up competitor B and, after turning B upside down, brought him down head first onto the hard surface. Permanent crippling or death was the common result of this pile-driving tactic.

## Precious Olive Oil

It takes the olive tree 16 years to bear fruit, and it takes 40 years before the tree and its fruit reach perfection. The government of Pisistratus subsidized large-scale introduction of olive trees during the sixth century B.C., and the destruction of olive orchards during the Peloponnesian War contributed heavily to Athenian decline.

For the Greeks, olive oil had many uses. The first pruning provided oil for eating, the second for anointing and skin care, the third for lamps, and the remaining for fuel. The crop proved so valuable in the Athenian economy that the state held a monopoly on all exports, for olive oil and wine alone carried sufficient value to pay for grains from the granaries of the ancient world.

## Bread, the Staple of Life

For any society in which the bulk of the population lives close to the poverty line, a substance as basic as bread is crucial to survival. When Victor Hugo's Jean Valjean committed the theft that made him a galley slave, in *Les Misérables*, he was not stealing cake. Athenian authorities regulated very strictly all supplies and movement of grains. No one could purchase more than 75 bushels on one occasion. A grain reserve was kept in the state-owned storehouses; in times of shortage it was placed in the market to prevent price fluctuations, and also to prevent fortunes from being made on a monopoly at the expense of public hunger. It was not by chance that in Egypt the pharaoh's priests were the custodians of the public granaries.

## The Importance of Feminine Beauty

The use of beauty aids was common among Greek women who could afford such things. Thick cork shoe soles were used to make one taller and padding embellished areas of the body that were lacking, while extra abundance was curtailed by tight lacing. Greek women even wore cloth brassieres. Both sexes used oils for hair and skin, and women often intertwined ribbons, beads, and jewelry into their braids. Plutarch (A.D. 46?–120?) commented on the degree of physical vanity, telling that an epidemic of suicide among the women of Miletus was abruptly halted by a simple regulation, which decreed that henceforth all self-slain women would be carried naked through the marketplace to their burial.

# The Status of the Greek Wife

Demosthenes wrote that it is quite acceptable for a man to have a concubine, for after all men need "concubines for the daily health of our bodies, and wives to bear us lawful offspring and to be the faithful guardians of our homes." So women of the classical age withstood a very conspicuous double standard, but also knew that the concubine, when her charms diminished, would end as a household slave; only the wife's offspring would be considered legitimate. However, adultery led to divorce if it was committed by the wife. In such a case the husband would be spoken of as "carrying horns," and the wife would be sent away.

# The Greek View of Love

The ancient Greeks believed that love between a man and a woman was essentially physical, hence episodic, and seldom a reason for marriage. Wives were for procreation and courtesans for recreational pleasure, while the kind of love that might cause in a man such feelings as passion, piety, ecstasy, jealousy, brooding, sleeplessness, or longing was generally reserved to relationships between males. It was frankly conceded by the Greek philosophers, Plato included, that love between man and man is nobler and more spiritual than love between man and woman. The feelings generated between man and woman could never be of the strength that compels a man to risk his life to save a comrade on the field of battle. This has led to the modern belief that Greek society was essentially homosexual, but not necessarily in the physical sense. After all, that is what the courtesans were for.

# Athenian Resistance to War

While Greek cities and resources were suffering from the deprivations of the Peloponnesian War, Aristophanes spoke out in the *Lysistrata* with a plea for peace. In this play, while the custodians of Athenian war policy are fast asleep, their wives gather at the Acropolis to discuss a means of bringing the war to an end. The wives decide to withhold the comforts and pleasures of love until their husbands agree to open peace negotiations and send an embassy of women to Sparta to induce a conciliatory response. The men awake, order their wives home; the women refuse with harsh words and defend their position with pails of hot water. The men insist that women have no business meddling in public matters, while the women retort that proof of their competence and resourcefulness is evident in their handling of their husbands' monies and managing of their homes. The men concede; Lysistrata arranges a peace conference while the wives ply delegates from both sides with plenty of wine. A treaty is signed and, it is assumed, the joys of love are restored.

## The Tragedy of Pericles

In 430 B.C., while Athens was locked in a struggle with Sparta, the great Athenian statesman Pericles (495?–429 B.C.) drew the people and troops of Attica within the walls of Athens in a strategic move that called for the navy to win the war. Unfortunately, the concentration of population soon led to the outbreak of a plague, which Lucretius (96–55 B.C.) tells us carried off one-fourth of the soldiers and many more civilians. As a result, Pericles was indicted for misuse of funds (he probably did bribe Spartan rulers), convicted, deposed from office, and fined. After his sister and his two legitimate sons had also died of the plague, and no better leader could be found, he was restored to power and citizenship was awarded his illegitimate son. Soon after, Pericles also died of the plague.

## The Shrewdness of Socrates

With the mention of ancient Greece no name comes more readily to mind than that of Socrates (469–399 B.C.). The specific charge that was made against the teacher of rhetoric reads: "A public offender in that he does not recognize, but introduces new demonical beings" and "he has also offended by corrupting the youth." This charge was rendered even more serious because at the time Athens was locked in a losing struggle with the Spartan league.

Socrates was condemned to death, but through the aid of bribes by friends he was offered the opportunity to escape to exile and live. He refused, possibly because he wished the responsibility for his death to rest squarely on his accusers. One of his loyal followers (as Plato tells us) exclaimed, "You die undeservedly!" Socrates, sophist to the end, responded, "Would you, then, have me deserve death?" For Socrates felt that he had but a few years left and these were the burdensome years of life when one faced the diminished faculties that come with age. If there was an afterlife, he was confident that he would be rewarded there because he had honestly and forthrightly sought truth while he lived; on the other hand, if the gods provided only nothingness after death, then he would enjoy the quietude of slumber. In contrast, two possibilities loomed large for those who had condemned him: How would the gods in the afterlife treat those who destroyed the search for truth, and did not the accusers also face the vicissitudes that Socrates had escaped?

## Alexander the Great

Recent scholarship on this great ancient ruler/conqueror (by historian John O'Brien) confirms that Alexander the Great (356–323 B.C.), by the years prior to his death at age 33, was an alcoholic. Most scholars, however, noting Alexander's respect for the lessons taught by Greek philosophers and dramatists, insist the condition was encouraged by retarded recovery from battle wounds, fatigue, and a fever that attacked his body during his last campaigns. Medical care was of course primitive; the most common form of battlefield anesthesia was mandragora juice.

It was indeed a sad decline for one who during his early twenties resented the time lost to essential sleep. Both Plutarch and Arrian tell of Alexander's reserved manner in the way of food and drink. He refused rich foods, resisted the services of famous chefs, and insisted that a night march provided a good appetite for breakfast, while a light breakfast enhanced the appetite for dinner. Alexander was equally reserved in his sexual activity, a condition no doubt influenced by his preoccupation with incessant activity. While he took many wives for reasons of state and politics, he preferred the company of generals. When an aide once brought a beautiful woman to his tent late at night, we are told by Plutarch that the youthful general asked her, "Why at this time?" She explained that she had to be certain her husband was asleep. After dismissing her quickly Alexander berated his servants for having contributed to his possible adultery.

## Hellenistic Extremes

The eastern empires that survived the era of Alexander the Great were plagued by nearly continuous warfare. The Hellenistic period has often been described as one of extremes, both positive and negative. On one hand, history witnessed the greatest individual fortunes ever amassed, the largest library collections, and the most populous cities, which had extensive engineers and equipment. On the other hand, the record shows great pillage, widespread poverty, and an increased practice of infanticide far exceeding that of most ancient societies. Symbolically, the frequent use of elephants in Hellenistic armies may have indicated a questionable value system. Though strong, useful, and impressive in size, in the military sense an elephant could be disabled by one small soldier, who could hack the leg tendons of the animal and render it no more than a worthless carcass.

## The Festival of Hanukkah

Through his culture and learning, Alexander the Great was Greek rather than Macedonian. His tutor was none other than Aristotle, and both would have agreed that to be culturally non-Greek was to be a barbarian. Hence Alexander, through his conquests of lands to the north and east of Egypt, was the true propagator of what we call the Hellenistic world, and his successors for centuries after his death (323 B.C.) attempted to continue the practice of hellenizing the Near East. That was exactly the aim of the Syrian ruler Antiochus IV (175–164 B.C.)—to wipe out, once and for all, the Jewish faith and supplant it with Zeus, Greek law, and Greek culture. In 165 B.C., however, a strong thrust by Hasidic (Pious Ones) Jews, led ably by Judas Maccabaeus and employing guerrilla tactics, seized Jerusalem and rededicated the Second

Temple, which had been desecrated by Antiochus three years earlier. Judas Maccabaeus tore down the altar of Zeus and won for the Jewish faith a degree of autonomy that would survive until Roman expansion into Jerusalem. The festival of Hanukkah celebrates this military victory and recalls the Talmud story of how a small amount of oil (enough for a single day) miraculously burned for a full eight days in the temple, until appropriate and consecrated oil could be found. Today, each December, Jews worldwide celebrate this historical event with the ceremonial lighting of candles over a period of eight days.

# ROME AND THE EMPIRE

## *The Lesson of Crucifixion*

Death on the cross was uniquely Roman. Crucifixion was deliberately a slow and agonizing ordeal, specifically intended to furnish the general populace with what modern educators would call a visual aid. The purpose of Roman law, and of the practices of Western Europe until well into the nineteenth century, was to publicly demonstrate the result of certain types of criminal conduct, in Latin *terrorum populi.*

In the case of crucifixion the victim, hanging by his hands and subject to respiratory failure and death within two hours, could avoid fainting and the consequent respiratory failure by supporting himself on a peg located in the vertical shaft of the cross. When pain to the bare feet ultimately became too severe, the victim might again permit his body to hang free. Oscillation from one state of pain to the other usually lasted for three days. Then, the Roman authorities would use a club to break the shin bones, rendering the use of the peg too painful. Death then came quickly of respiratory and heart failure. From the records of Jesus' death, there is no reason to believe that any of the three crosses included pegs or that death was purposely prolonged.

In the first century A.D., Spartacus, an ex-slave and gladiator, led a slave uprising that ravaged much of the Italian countryside for nearly two years. The 6,000 captured followers of Spartacus were crucified along the Appian Way, the Roman highway leading south from the capital to Brindisi, so that citizen masters might take comfort and slaves take heed.

## The Baths of Rome

Romans who could afford the time and effort have had no rivals, ancient or modern, who matched their concern for cleanliness or appreciation of the bath. If one had a home the bathtub was likely a part of it, and spacious, elaborate bathing fixtures graced the homes of the wealthy. Many thousands made the public bath a part of their daily routine and several emperors contributed government funds to the expansion of bathing accommodations. By the time of Tiberius (A.D. 14–37) there were 170 private baths in Rome. By the death of Constantine (337) there were nearly 900 such baths and another 1,300 public swimming pools.

However, all of these facilities were surpassed by the great state-managed public baths, which were staffed by slaves. Able to provide hot water, public baths were erected from the time of Jesus through the reign of Constantine. Built of mortared brick and marble, these baths accommodated from 1,600 to several thousand bathers at once. Admission fees were within reach of nearly all inhabitants; there were two six-hour shifts for women and the same for men. There were also adjoining exercise areas, arranged competitions, and slaves available to massage the bodies of patrons. There were several sauna-like rooms for soothing the pain of arthritis and rheumatism. Other services and facilities included treatments, rubbings with oil, rest areas for table games, and rooms for reading or conversation.

## Rome's Legacy

A good deal of the aspects of our modern society that we take for granted were actually first established and spread by the Roman Empire. In the United States, we travel nationwide with the confidence that roads are in good repair, that emergency aid is available, and that both a marriage license and a driver's license are respected in all states of the United States and Canada. A letter can be mailed in any location for the same price and with the assumption it will reach its destination within a reasonable time.

As has been emphasized by Edward Gibbon and many more modern historians, a Roman citizen in about A.D. 100 could send a message from Rome to London in 28 days. In 1834, it took Britain's Robert Peel 30 days to cover the same ground in a serious hurry. Apart from written documents and couriers, the empire sent messages across Europe even more rapidly using Signal Corps–type flagmen stationed on appropriate mountaintops. This practice was copied 17 centuries later by one of Rome's admirers: Napoleon Bonaparte. In the city of Rome itself, two shifts of 70,000 each served those wishing to use the public baths; a fresh and pure water supply was delivered to all the cities of the empire through a carefully engineered system of aqueducts. Many of the aqueducts still stand today in such removed areas as Nimes, France, and Segovia, Spain. Roman roads, often paved, fanned out to render easy travel as far as the Danube, the Rhine, the hinterland of North Africa, and the Black Sea. Romans dined on more than a dozen varieties of olives from as far away as Persia, wore the wool of England, drank the wine of Spain, and observed the tragedies performed by touring Greek players. Pirates had been cleared from the Mediterranean, and thousands safely traveled throughout the area on ships with sails and oars laden with thousands of tons of goods moving east, west, north, or south. Edward Gibbon was a contemporary of such men as Benjamin Franklin and George Washington, yet, in his view, based on conditions observed in his day, there was no better time to have lived in all history than between A.D. 96 and 180. Citizens of the Roman Empire enjoyed the greatest prosperity, security, and comfort of any population in history.

## Rome's Great Buildings

The Coliseum has come to be regarded as the largest of Roman structures. However, it is only the largest that visibly remains, and its remains are only leftovers from 19 centuries of scavenging for other construction. Probably the largest Roman building, Julius Caesar's Circus Maximus amphitheater, could accommodate 180,000 spectators. The amphitheater was furnished mostly with wooden seats that were converted to marble by the emperor

Trajan (A.D. 98–117). By comparison, the Coliseum seated a mere 50,000. The Circus Maximus was decorated with statuary and varied works of art and possessed no less than 80 entrances and exits. Like the baths, these large Roman structures were designed to provide service on a grand scale for the greatest number in the largest empire the world had ever known.

## Roman Contraception, Abortion, Infanticide

The first century A.D. witnessed a strong trend among the wealthier classes of Rome to discourage marriage and legitimate procreation. Juvenal, Petronius, Seneca, and Pliny the Elder all chronicled this development. Contraception was practiced in mechanical ways as well as chemical ones. A common form of the latter was applying heavy oil or cedar gum to the male organ before coitus to guard against conception. And though both moral teachers and the law stood opposed to abortion, the prosperous practiced it widely through the use of drugs or female abortion specialists. Juvenal flippantly advised the Roman husband to judge favorably his wife's desire for an abortion: After all, she might very likely give birth to an Ethiopian. Infanticide was practiced throughout the ancient world by nearly all civilized societies. During the first century A.D. in Rome, unwanted babies were often left at the base of the Columna Lactoria (so named because the state provided the nurses to save them), to die of exposure or be claimed by wives who could not bear children.

## Vespasian: Emperor of Heavy Taxes

Emperor Vespasian (A.D. 69–79), a rough, forceful man of modest birth who had a long and successful military career, was already 60 when he seized the reins of Roman imperial power to end the chaos that followed the death of Nero. He was practical and did not abuse his position for personal or family gratification. Suetonius tells us that Vespasian determined that 40 billion sesterces were needed to pay off the government's debts. He sought every means to increase revenue, even going so far as to place a tax on the use of public latrines, of which the capital had an abundance. When his son, Titus, who had established his own military reputation during the ruthless war against the Jews, protested such an improper source of revenue, Vespasian merely held some coins under the youth's nose and asked if there was any obnoxious odor.

## The Importance of the Roman Games

Contests, competitions, and games were held for various reasons ranging from festivals for the gods to honoring heroic dead. Most of these contests were held in stadiums, and though sports from the Olympic Games in Greece were sometimes included, the Roman public had become accustomed to the blood and gory death associated with the popular gladiatorial exhibitions. Boxing, which Virgil described in his *Aeneid*, was popular with the Romans, but Roman boxing gloves had thick, metal reinforcements across the knuckles.

Few competitions were more popular than the races at the Circus Maximus, where 180,000 fans sporting their teams' colors would crowd into the giant hippodrome much the way soccer fans do today. More exciting than the jockey-ridden horse races were the seven-lap contests of chariots pulled by four horses abreast. Rich backers funded teams from rival stables much as companies now support cars in the Indianapolis 500. Vendors sold their wares, prostitutes prospered, and betting added to the anxiety of the spectators. The crucial moments of each race, of which there might be 20 per day, came in the turns that all chariots had to make at each end of the stadium. As the speed increased, leads changed, the turf became more treacherous, and the slave charioteers tired. The danger and anticipation of disaster amid clashing men, animals, and equipment mounted, and the roar of the crowd could be heard for miles.

## Bishop Polycarp, Martyr

Persecution of Christians during the first and second centuries A.D. was somewhat sporadic, often the result of an emperor's whim or the regional vitality of the subversive faith. In Smyrna, during the reign of Antonius, the populace demanded that the local Roman administrator enforce the law against the traitorous religion. But even after the execution of 11 Christians in the amphitheater the bloodthirstiness of the crowd was not sated. They clamored for the death of the local Christian bishop, Polycarp, who was well known in the community owing to his 86 years and his saintly demeanor. Polycarp was hunted down and brought to the arena, where the Roman authorities demanded that he "take the oath, revile Christ, and we will let you go." As recorded in the *Acts of the Martyrs*, the good bishop replied, "For eighty-six years have I been his servant, and he has done me no wrong; how then can I blaspheme my king who saved me?" The mob demanded Polycarp be burned alive, but the flames refused to burn him. His form remained intact and gave off the fragrance of expensive incense, while the crowd demanded that the executioner do more. The *Acts* reports that when he was subsequently stabbed a dove was released from his body, followed by so much blood that the fire was quenched.

# The Contrasts of Caesar Augustus

Caesar Augustus almost seems to have been two different people. As a youth, the impetuous Octavian was merciless and often egotistical, engaged in various sexual indulgences, calmly observed Cicero's head hanging in the Forum, and was a cohort of Mark Antony and a collaborator with a sequence of selfish factions. He contested both Antony and Cleopatra for rule of the Roman Empire, and eventually presided over the destruction of both. By his mid-30s, however, Caesar Augustus was a man nearly physically broken by the domestic and foreign rigors of his life. He was nervous and plagued by kidney stones, typhus, and rheumatism, but had reached the pinnacle of individual political power. He did not abuse his power, but lived another 40 years as an example of justice, moderation, fidelity, generosity, and toleration. He confined his diet to simple foods like bread, fish, cheese, and fruit, merely observing while others enjoyed the rich culinary delights of his banquets. Even Cleopatra could not tempt Caesar Augustus.

## Pontius Pilate and Jesus

Apart from the accounts preserved in the Synoptic Gospels and the passing references of the historians Josephus and Tacitus, there are few details about the death of Jesus. But Roman administrative records do tell of Pontius Pilate, procurator of Judea. This position was a lower rank than governor, and any Roman bureaucrat would have considered service in Judea undesirable. To say that the Jews were always revolting would merely have been a bad Roman pun. Pilate wanted his geographical turnip to bleed wealth and lie still. He in fact despised the inhabitants of Judea. Thus, if Jesus was a thorn in the side of the leaders of the Jewish community, it brought only pleasure to Pilate. It was only when these leaders pointed out that the followers of Jesus called him a king that Pilate took notice. Pilate knew that Emperor Tiberius, a most suspicious and vindictive ruler, might take severe action against a Roman administrator who permitted another would-be monarch to roam unrestrained. After questioning Jesus, Pilate found no reason to sentence him, but simply gave him over to the soldiers to do with as they might. The crown of thorns was an act of mockery, a display to show all what should be the state of the "king of the Jews." Pilate merely followed the path of least resistance in dealing with Jesus.

## Roman Suicide

While it may never be known what form of suicide was most common in the Roman world, the one most often described in records of the era is slashing the veins of the wrist. When the powerful found themselves on the losing side of a struggle or of the will of Caesar, suicide would be the first choice or, in effect, a sentence. Tacitus says that Nero ordered the philosopher Seneca "to die." Both the sage and his wife opened their veins while sitting in a large bath of warm water. If the instrument was especially sharp, the death was without serious pain, and suicide removed the possibility for others to gain personal satisfaction by assassinating the condemned person.

# Gluttony among the Rich

"They eat to vomit, and vomit to eat" was a sentiment expressed by Seneca, first-century A.D. scholar-philosopher and sometime advisor to Emperor Nero. It refers to the exceptional cases of gluttony on the part of some of Rome's ill-mannered ultra rich. The strong element of truth behind this statement is confirmed by the ostentatious display provided the guests of the ex-slave and millionaire Trimalchio at a banquet described in Petronius' *Satyricon*. From appetizer to dessert, pampered guests might enjoy rare birds, fish, fruit, mullets, eel, snails, ostrich wings, flamingo tongues, and goose and pork livers. Custom permitted the diner to empty his stomach (by use of an emetic) as often as he might desire, so he could richly attack each delicacy with new-found hunger. The availability and affordability of such rare morsels is significant proof of Roman economic prosperity and sophistication.

# Caligula and Nero

The long list of men who held Rome's imperial throne, as well as the women who surrounded them, provides history with a selection of conspicuous contrasts. Even more intriguing to the student of the Roman Empire are the reigns of two of the worst monsters ever to fill the imperial office, because despite both of them the empire continued to grow in size, prosperity, and dynamic civil accomplishment. The conduct of these two emperors was recorded by a contemporary "keyhole peeker" and energetic gossip, Suetonius; by the great historian, Roman Senator Tacitus; and by Dio Cassius. Tacitus is known to have hated emperors but also to have been a good historian, while Dio Cassius lived two centuries after the events he chronicled. Neither chose to dispute the validity of the traditional accounts, which reveal the cruel conduct of the two rulers.

## Caligula

Gaius Caesar Germanicus (ruled A.D. 37–41), known to history as Caligula (which means Little Boot), commenced his reign with the amenities—pardons, gifts, lowering of taxes, and forgiving of many debts—that often marked the style of a new potentate, and within a very short time became a power-hungry, egotistical, petty despot. This tall, huge, hairy man with sunken eyes was given to practicing hideous expressions in the mirror. He often reminded banquet guests that he could have them all killed where they reclined, and was known to calmly report to wife or mistress during an embrace that she would lose her beautiful head whenever he chose to order it.

Among the many recorded charges against Caligula are the following:

1. He lived in incest with his sisters out of admiration for the customs of Egyptian pharaohs, and forced one sister to divorce her husband, after which he treated her as though she were his lawful wife.

2. Government funds were lavished upon fancy balls, banquets, palatial gardens, and royal barges, causing a reduction of government subsidies of the crucial grain supply and thereby subjecting much of the capital's populace to famine. Donations to favored charioteers and gambling losses merely added to the problem. The emperor also had a marble stall with ivory manger built for his own race horse, Incinatus, invited the horse to dinner, and even proposed to make the animal a consul of the empire.

3. The earnings of prostitutes were taxed for each amorous act, from the first embrace on, and many rich men were condemned to death on a false charge of treason so that Caligula might enjoy both their fortunes and their wives.

4. After detecting a conspiracy against him, Caligula revealed his true penchant for sadism. He demanded that the conspirators be executed in the slowest and most painful way possible. According to Suetonius, he even had bald-headed prisoners fed to animals for the public good.

By the age of 29, Caligula was a wretch worn beyond his years by his own indulgence. A tribune of his own guard, incensed by the obscenities that the emperor used as passwords, murdered him in a palace hallway; soon after, Caligula's wife and daughter were also brutally slain, as if to halt the breed.

# Nero

Lucius Nero (ruled A.D. 54–68), though he gained the throne by usurping the better claims of Britannicus and because his mother, Agrippina, poisoned Emperor Claudius, offered five years of stable and considerate administration, aided by able counsel. If we considered only the first five years of Nero's reign, we would talk of well-guarded frontiers, the removal of pirates, expansion and peace in Parthia and Armenia, and a general growth of efficient, honest, frugal bureaucracy in a prosperous economy with declining taxes. Thus, the explosion of brutal megalomania and self-adulation that filled the next nine years, at least at the top level of power, offers shocking contrast not only to the first five years, but also to the general trends throughout the Mediterranean area. Nero would have been the tabloids' dream, at least in the area of personal whims and excesses. Let us consider the following list:

1. Despite an education that afforded him the benefit of the stoic Seneca as tutor, Nero developed no discernible appreciation or particular respect for philosophy, codes of morality, or religion. Suetonius asserted that Nero had only contempt for all cults and that the only goddess for whom he ever expressed respect was the one on whose image he chose to urinate.

2. In diet, sexual behavior, and entertainment, he was given to the gross or extreme. Nero disguised himself to seek the thrills of Roman nightlife with cohorts of like mind and temperament, sampling cheap brothels and taverns. He also took advantage of group anonymity while robbing shops, abusing women, or, as Dio Cassius says, "practicing lewdness on boys he met to the point of wounding or even murdering them."

3. Nero's liaison with Poppea Sabina, a young woman of fine beauty but also great conceit, led to tragedy for others on several fronts. Not only did he assign her husband to administer the province we know as Portugal, but also followed Poppea's demands to divorce his wife, Octavia, so that he could marry her instead. The madness of Nero's infatuation ultimately led to his commissioned murder (after three attempts) of his mother, the very woman who had poisoned Emperor Claudius and thereby provided her son with rule over the only civilized, known world. In raw fashion Nero's agents pursued his mother to her villa in the last of the three tries,

listened to her plea, then dispatched her with a sword. Observing the naked body, Nero was reported to have said that he did not realize he had such a beautiful mother.

4. While he is to be commended and respected for both the appreciation and participation he exhibited in the areas of painting, sculpture, music, and poetry, Nero degraded the imperial office by hunting for public applause when he appeared as a performer; in the midst of his performing zeal, he even had himself deified.

5. According to Tacitus, the emperor caused a fire that ruined half of Rome, which he wished to renovate to his liking, then unjustifiably blamed and persecuted a group known as Christians for the supposed crimes.

6. Nero was charged by historians with the death of a pregnant Poppea from a kick in the stomach, and went on to have a youth who resembled Poppea castrated so that he might use the boy in every way like a woman.

7. Nipping in the bud a supposed plot against him, Nero carried out a tortuous blood bath against many of the senatorial class and other elite of Rome and, having achieved what he deemed adequate security, then left for a performance tour of Greece to show the world the talents he possessed. Because he rescinded taxes wherever he performed, the applause and acceptance grew, all became solicitous, and because he was the emperor he won first prize in all competitions, from athletic games to singing, acting, or harp playing. He returned to Rome displaying 1,808 prizes.

Finally, several generals rose in revolt against this freak of an emperor. Nero fled the capital, went into hiding, and ultimately chose suicide, but could not even carry off this last act with any finesse. After all, the point of the blade is sharp; it pricks. Eventually, as the assassins closed in, a slave had to aid him with the blade. History records that his last words were, "What an artist dies in me!"

## Commodus: Brute, Freak, or Champion?

As with both Caligula and Nero, we must depend upon "tradition" for much of our knowledge of the behavior of Commodus. Most scribes, such as Tacitus and Dio Cassius, wrote from the bias of their class or position and appear to have been offended by the conduct of many who filled the imperial throne. Of Commodus, who became emperor at age 19, we learn that he was unsurpassed in skill with both sword and bow, that he often fought publicly against a hippopotamus, an elephant, or a tiger, and that in a single exhibition he killed 100 tigers with exactly 100 arrows. His string of gladiatorial combats supposedly reached more than 1,000 without a defeat, and he remained undefeated in an even longer string of wrestling competitions. Commodus drank and gorged to excess, ostentatiously spent state funds, enjoyed a harem that included 300 boys and 300 women, and often chose to engage in the "sexually explicit." He is known for a long list of varied cruelties that appear to have grown out of a combination of ego, megalomania, and religious hatred. One of his most bizarre behaviors was to assume the identity of Hercules. Garbed in skins, Commodus would mount his chariot and surge among the Roman populace, indiscriminately bashing unlucky bystanders with his "club of Hercules."

Commodus placed subordinates in charge of executing his daily duties, so as to enjoy more time for competitions and the applause of the crowds, thereby subjecting hundreds of Rome's elite class to the brutality and corruption of his dictatorial aides. The last of these lieutenants, along with the emperor's mistress, Marcia, decided to end the reign of terror once and for all. After the cup of poison Marcia gave Commodus worked too slowly, his wrestling partner conveniently strangled him in his bath. According to another account, Narcissus snapped his neck; the emperor was dead at age 31.

## *Roman Admiration of Teutonic Virility*

The Roman historian Tacitus (A.D. 55–118), our primary source for information about the barbarian tribes that existed beyond the empire's northern frontiers, backhandedly criticized the tendency toward comfort and luxury he saw about him in Rome, in his apparently approving description of Germanic warrior life, of the warriors' unbending loyalty to their chieftains, and especially of Germanic audacity in the face of conspicuous danger. The most weighty example he provides of this audacity, quite apart from any zeal in the heat of battle, is simply the Teutons' willingness to seek challenges of all types, regardless of the price. According to Tacitus, the Germanic warrior was even eager to stake his life on a single roll of dice.

## A Lesson on Sin

Saint Augustine (354–430), a seminal theological scholar and an early father of the medieval Church, left us his *Confessions* in addition to other major works. In the *Confessions*, the saint revealed in detail how, during his youth, he and a friend had worked concertedly to scale a high wall separating his family's property from that of a neighbor, so as to steal pears. But Augustine continues his account, his aim being to teach a lesson rather than to merely report his violation of a single commandment. He goes on to say that his family had a large pear orchard of their own, and that these pears were far superior to the ones that he and his friend stole. By telling this story, Augustine was illustrating the powerful drive to sin. For him and his friend, it was the desire to sin that drove them to steal something that was inferior to what they already had. Thus, in Saint Augustine's view, humans must be constantly diligent to resist the weaknesses that have become their ever-present burden since the Fall from the Garden of Eden.

## The Sacking of Rome

A horde of Thracian Goths led by Alaric camped at the gates of Rome in 408; it took a ransom of 5,000 pounds of gold, 30,000 pounds of silver, thousands of silk and animal-skin tunics, and 3,000 pounds of spices to placate the invaders. But in 410, provoked by a broken treaty, Alaric and his Goths, aided by some Hunnic forces, seized the city by storm. For three days Rome was subjected to indiscriminate pillage: thousands were murdered, women were raped, and thousands of prisoners were taken. Works of art made from gold or silver were melted down for the metal, and masterpieces were destroyed. Then Alaric restored discipline and led his troops south on an expedition to conquer Sicily. Later that year he was stricken with a fever and died at

Cosenza. Slaves were forced to divert the flow of the Busento River to clear proper ground for his grave. Then the river was returned to its previous course to provide constant security for the dead leader's resting place, and, as extra insurance, the slaves who had performed the labors were slain.

## Papal Instructions for Missionaries

As pope, Gregory the Great (590–604) was directly responsible for the successful mission that delivered Roman Christianity to England. Tradition tells of his strong curiosity about bondsmen and slaves he had observed who were from that far-off northern land. Pope Gregory commissioned an expedition successfully led by Augustine of Canterbury, who converted King Ethelbert and soon brought his subjects into the Roman flock. But most interesting about this undertaking were the methods Pope Gregory authorized to induce the conversion to Christianity.

Augustine was ordered to build religious structures for worship at the very locations where pagan rituals were known to take place. If the pagans worshiped a mother goddess figure, then Augustine was to concentrate on the role of the Virgin Mary and the Immaculate Conception. If, instead, they worshiped a large retinue of lesser gods (e.g., identified with natural phenomenon), then the focus would be placed on the great deeds of the apostles, saints, and other stalwarts of Roman Christian history, including the intercession of saints for the troubled faithful.

Thus, by a combination of adaptation and ritualistic assimilation, Pope Gregory set a successful pattern for the future work of missionaries who would carry the "true faith" north to Scandinavia and east to Poland.

## The Valuable Color Purple

The student of the politics that surrounded the Roman and Byzantine emperors, their families, and the fratricidal struggles to seize or retain the imperial thrones, often runs into the phrase *born under the purple*. It was during this historical period that biological legitimacy was tied to a specific color, in this case the official color of emperors in various arenas and, particularly, the color of imperial garments.

Difficulties in acquiring and preserving the dye for purple made cloth of that color the most expensive; therefore, purple appropriately became the color of royalty and status. The precise name for the color was Tyrian purple, because the dye came from an indigo derivative extracted from mollusks found along the Levantine coastal regions around the port of Tyre. When the color was used in political terms it indicated direct lineage of imperial blood, a factor that was profoundly important in marriage treaties or alliances, that determined succession to the throne, and that, in the case of a coup d'etat, made it necessary to eliminate any possible rival born under the purple. One unverified story of the tenth century has it that Byzantine Emperor Nicephorus II Phocas duped Otto I of Germany, because the daughter Nicephorus offered as wife to the future Otto II, Theophano, was not born under the purple.

# CHAPTER II

# The Medieval World

The term *Middle Ages* is no doubt one of the most generously inclusive chronological designations used by historians. This period includes developments in the eastern, western, and northern reaches of Europe beginning with the barbarian invasions and the career of Saint Augustine through the birth of the Renaissance in Florence (1300) and the close of the English War of the Roses (1485). Clearly, the Middle Ages incorporates very diverse events and institutions. At the start of this period, Roman imperial authority collapsed in the west, giving rise to successor states: Frankish Gaul, Visigothic Spain, and Anglo-Saxon England, with only the papacy as a weak centerpoint. At the same time the eastern Roman Empire, its capital Byzantine Constantinople, lived on until 1453 as a sophisticated commercial state. The more vital signs of civilization (commerce, coinage, cities) passed through an era of near stagnation in the west during the Dark Ages (c. 500s–1000s) and re-awakened around 1100. This re-awakening brought the growth of trade and towns, several religious crusades to the Near East, the construction of cathedrals, and the development of centralizing institutions in law and government. Meanwhile, the papacy rose to the pinnacle of its power by the Fourth Lateran Council of 1215. The Middle Ages also saw philosophy and theology mature from the early works of Boethius, to Saint Augustine, to a Carolingian renaissance, to the intellectual contexts of the twelfth century (Abelard), and finally to the reassured approach and conclusions of Saint Thomas Aquinas. Feudalism lost the constitutional struggle for jurisdiction to national monarchy, uniformity of law, and the rise of a merchant class. These merchants demanded recognition of their cities and laws to protect their commercial activities. The international authority of the Universal Church that was felt both in the secular hierarchy and through monastic houses in every geographical corner, was likewise weakened by economic changes, and also by the growing power of the "state" as manifested in the monarchy and by a trend toward clerical worldliness. The fourteenth century was indeed as calamitous as historian Barbara Tuchman has asserted (*A Distant Mirror: The Calamitous 14th Century,* 1978). This century saw a shift of the papacy to Avignon, first two and ultimately three competing popes, the worst years of the Hundred Years' War, and repeated visits by the Black Death from 1348–1400. Yet, out of all this came a quickening that led to the rise of modern capitalism, world discovery, the invention of moveable type, a religious revolution, and the state system centered around great cities, which still characterizes modern times.

## Questions for Discussion

- How comfortable was life at home for one who was lord of a castle? What might you eat in the way of hot food at the castle's main table?

- What were the interesting attributes of Theodora, the most famous of eastern Roman (Byzantine) empresses?

- What impression did the supposedly splendorous imperial court at Constantinople make on Bishop Liutprand of Cremona?

- What dangers did religious pilgrims or crusaders face along their route to Spain, apart from military activities?

- Why might authorities wait for a long period before burying a king (for example, King Henry I in 1135)?

- For what reasons might historians claim that Saint Francis of Assisi was not only the ideal friar of the Middle Ages, but also, after his full conversion, possibly the most Christlike figure to walk the earth since the short mission of Jesus?

- Were Jews persecuted during the Middle Ages? Why?

- What features of Anglo-Saxon law prevented blood feuds or attempts at revenge?

- In what fashion did legal procedures, including trial by combat, provide for decisions rendered by God, not by man?

- On what occasion did Edward I of England create the title that is still reserved for the heir to the English throne?

- Is it inaccurate to describe student life around the year 1200 with terms such as serenity, quietude, and contemplation?

- How did students employ their language skills in ways other than the serious study of theology?

- Joan of Arc was the great heroine of the Hundred Years' War, but was ultimately tried and executed for sorcery. In addition to the criminal charges against her, what other facts regarding her conduct worked against her during her trial in Rouen, France?

## The Life of the Huns

The Huns were warlike and ferocious conquerors who moved westward from Asia into Europe, plundering and causing the relocation of many other great peoples in their wake. The Huns' drives stimulated the other major barbarian movements of the fourth and fifth centuries. The Huns were essentially an example of historian Arnold Toynbee's "arrested culture," a basically quasi-nomadic horseback culture. Their warriors, employing swift travel over long distances, often kept extra horses with them to ride as each horse became exhausted. They regularly slept and ate in their primitive saddles. To provide solid protein for food, they placed strips of raw meat under their saddles so that the salty perspiration of the horses would cure and preserve the meat for future meals.

## Laxity and Decline in Monastic Orders

One reason for a number of monastic revivals during the Middle Ages was the simple fact that laxity and corruption had increased among members of the regular orders. Among Benedictines, both the Cluniac and Cistercian orders were developed as revivals and expansions of the monastic ideals and organization. From the meager beginnings of a single house at Citeaux in 1098, the Cistercians numbered 343 houses by the death of their leader, Saint Bernard of Clairvaux, in 1153, and before the end of the thirteenth century there were nearly 700 houses. However, despite their vows of poverty, the largest wool-producing agency of all of England by 1300 was the Cistercian order. This brings to mind a story related by historian G. G. Coulton about a monastery in which the brothers adhered strictly to their own local regulations and confined their consumption of wine to a single goblet per day. As it happens, the goblets in that monastery held two liters.

## Dining at the Castle Table

The knight or gentleman, sitting down to a meal in his castle in the eleventh century, most likely used no plate. Instead, stewed meat and vegetables were ladled onto a large plate-sized slice of black bread. When he had finished the stew (which he ate with his hands), he could then eat the gravy-soaked "plate." It is very likely that the only rule of table manners that was rigidly followed was that of not putting one's feet on the table until all had finished eating.

## Castle Floor Coverings

To reduce the damp chill of castle rooms, tapestries were often hung on the walls and reeds from river banks were strewn on the stone floors. One can imagine, when the reeds were removed in the spring, just how many meat bones and particles of dog dung had become part of the floor covering.

## Odor and the Medieval Town

The medieval traveler usually knew he was approaching a town while he was still a considerable distance away: He could smell it.

In medieval towns, refuse was simply thrown into the streets, and center ditches contained the contents of chamber pots, which were emptied from second-story windows. Hogs rooted here and there with chickens and dogs. Outside the town's gates (which were locked at sunset) the traveler might see one or more human carcasses hanging from a gibbet. These were the remains of convicted felons and served as a reminder to all visitors as to how they should conduct themselves while in that town.

## The Weight of Medieval Armor

By the beginning of the fourteenth century, armor had become so sophisticated that the properly equipped knight was literally encased in metal from the top of his head all the way to his toes. Even his horse might be partially shielded by armor. Of course, the weight of a full suit of armor also increased proportionally, and left the mounted knight less effective in battle. Before helmets were appropriately contoured to the head, a glancing blow from a lance might leave the eye opening facing to the rear.

To prepare for battle, the knight, a page, and two horses found a strong tree limb, over which a rope would be thrown and attached to the fully armored warrior. The rope was then tied under his arms while the page tied the other end to the second horse, which lofted the knight high enough so he could be lowered onto the stronger of the two animals. Once unhorsed in battle, a knight might not even be able to sit upright, leaving him defenseless against capture, victim to the jabs of a thin stiletto inserted through the cracks in his armor, or, if knocked unconscious, subject to suffocation if it was a hot August day. For armored cavalry, the Hundred Years' War (1338–1453) was a military disaster.

## Pilgrimages to Spain

The most visited, and hence most revered, shrine for the faithful of western Europe during the Middle Ages was that of Santiago de Compostela in northwestern Spain. From the north and east, most pilgrims journeyed to southwestern France, crossed the

Pyrenees through the area made famous by the *Song of Roland,* at Roncesvalles, descended the slopes to the Spanish city of Pamplona, and then pursued a winding course across northern Spain (Burgos, Leon) through the western reaches of the Cantabrians. There the pilgrims would humble themselves before the remains of the apostle James in the crypt of one of the most opulently decorated cathedrals in all of Europe. There is no precise information about the number of pilgrims who set out in such fashion, still less about the number who were robbed, beaten, or lost along the way, but it is known that a retinue of con artists regularly "worked" the route to relieve the naive of their worldly goods.

## *The* Song of Roland: *Some Facts, Much Fiction*

In alliance with some Muslim factions in northern Spain, the great Frankish ruler Charlemagne directed a two-pronged expedition south of the Pyrenees in 778. Gerona in the east and Pamplona farther west were taken, and siege was laid to Saragossa. After months without success the emperor and his forces retreated back to France through the pass in the Pyrenees at Roncesvalles. It was there, taking advantage of the lay of the land and light armor, that Christian Basque brigands treacherously ambushed the Frankish rear guard and supply wagons. The supplies were pillaged and the Frankish troops slaughtered. In the words of Charlemagne's court chronicler, Einhard, in his *Vita Caroli,* "In action were killed Eggihard the king's semeshal, Anselm count of the palace, and Roland duke of the marches of Brittany, together with a great many more."

These simple historical facts supplied the basic substance for one of the great literary pieces of the entire Middle Ages, one of France's greatest literary treasures, and a crucial link in the evolution of the French language between the eighth and the twelfth centuries—the *Song of Roland.* It was an epic, a *chanson de geste* (song of deeds), verbally recounted and embellished again and again over more than three centuries. By the twelfth century, when it was first presented in written form, the *Song of Roland* included all the ingredients of feudal ranks, chivalrous obligations, Christian duties and mission (it appeared just after the First Crusade), and the defense of the Christian West against the infidel Saracens. While Einhard could have known little of the battle's actual details, the later reader of the *chanson de geste* learns the names of dozens of French warriors, and even the names of their horses and swords. The sword of Roland (Durendal, which means "enduring") is even reported to contain holy Christian relics in its hilt. Archbishop Turpin slays thousands of Saracens, wielding his sword much like the blades of a modern helicopter, before he falls in the knightly and Christian cause. Meanwhile, Roland, out of a combination of dedication, pride, chivalrous virtue, and adventurous valor, fights until life's crimson fluid is flowing from his body before blowing the horn (named Oliphant) that could bring reinforcements to relieve his embattled troops.

Ultimately, in the full blossom of chivalrous romance, the news of the death of her beloved and betrothed Roland reaches "sweet" Aude at the palace of Charlemagne. She becomes pale, faints at the king's feet, and "dies forthwith." No student of the Middle Ages should miss the opportunity of comparing the events of 778 with the masterpiece so regularly studied in literature classes today.

# Was There a Real Robin Hood?

There is no concrete evidence regarding the activities of anyone called Robin Hood, who robbed from the rich and gave to the poor, during the time that Prince John of England abused both royal authority and the people while his brother Richard the Lion-Hearted was involved in the Third Crusade (1190–1199). However, the substance from one century can be and has been imposed on the history of another, as with the written version of the *Song of Roland* from c. 1100, which was based upon an expedition that occurred under the leadership of Charlemagne in 778. Historian Charles L. Tipton, a fourteenth-century specialist, indicates that English records for the fourteenth century reveal the activities of one Robin of Hoade, who carried out his acts of banditry in the region known as Sherwood Forest.

## Viewing the Remains of the King

It has nearly always been customary for an important dignitary to lie in state after death so that all who wished to could pay their last respects. This, for many, might be an unpleasant occasion; as medieval practices afforded none of the bodily preparations that took place in ancient Egypt and are the practice today, it could actually be quite noisome. This was the case after the death of England's King Henry I Beauclerc, who died in 1135. Such a point was finally reached, as his remains were removed up cathedral steps for another round of visitations, when a foul-smelling fluid dripped from one corner of the coffin. The local bishop at once insisted that it was time for this man to be in the ground.

## Theodora, Justinian's Temptress Empress

In his *Buildings,* the Byzantine historian Procopius describes the wife of the great Emperor Justinian (527–565) as so beautiful that "to express her loveliness in words, or to portray it as a statue, would be altogether impossible for a mere human being." In his private and unpublished (at that time) "Secret History," however, he offers a candid discussion of Theodora's early life and character that borders on the purely malicious. Here we find a woman born and raised in the circus atmosphere of her bear-trainer father, eventually becoming an actress/prostitute who was given to abortions and who also gave birth to an illegitimate child. She later became the mistress of a Syrian tradesman, accompanying him to Alexandria, after which she "worked her way back" to Constantinople. We know only that she was a wool spinner when Justinian met and fell in love with her and made her his mistress, and ultimately his wife and empress.

She shared equally with her husband in the powers of the imperial office. She made and unmade popes and bishops, conducted diplomacy, set religious policy, and in her old age founded on the banks of the Bosporus a "convent of repentance" for reformed prostitutes.

# Political Brutality in Merovingian Gaul

During the sixth and seventh centuries, the rivalries between rulers of the two divisions of northern Gaul, and between the rulers and leading members of the aristocracy, offer some very dark pages in politics. For nearly all details we are dependent upon the words of Bishop Gregory of Tours (c. 540–594) in his *History of the Franks*. Essentially, the pretext for a series of civil wars was the subdivision of the Frankish realm among the four sons of Chlotar I in 561, but the most dynamic characters proved to be two women driven by a poisonous hatred of each other. One of the sons, Sigebert of Austrasia, married a Visigothic princess named Brunhilde whom the poet Venatius Fortunatus described as "most fair to look upon."

Soon afterward a second dream girl from Visigothic Spain became the wife of Sigebert's brother Chilperic, king of Neustria. She was none other than Brunhilde's sister, Galswintha. In order to marry her, however, Chilperic was forced to cast aside a cunning and cruel mistress named Fredegund. Shortly thereafter, Galswintha was found murdered, and though all fingers pointed properly to Fredegund, Chilperic married his former mistress. For this Brunhilde swore unrelenting vengeance and provoked war between Neustria and Austrasia. The struggle lasted until both queens were dead.

Fredegund employed various sinister tactics, the most common of which were poison and the dagger, often wielded by lower clergy. She even had the bishop of Rouen assassinated on the high altar, and one report says she personally attempted to take the life of her own daughter, Rigunth, by closing her head in a large chest to strangle her.

Fredegund died before she could murder Brunhilde, who went on to manipulate sons and grandsons in wars against each other for a decade. Finally, the nobles of Austrasia, Neustria, and Burgundy formed an alliance to rid themselves of this bloody and power-hungry queen. They defeated and strangled two of her grandsons and then, as we are told in the *Cambridge Medieval History*, "Brunhild herself was tortured for three days, set upon a camel as a mark of derision, and then tied by her hair, one arm, and one foot, to the tail of a vicious horse, which was then lashed to a fury." Obviously the civilizing and humanizing aspects of Christian teachings had made little headway among the political powers of seventh-century France.

## Clergy at War and Church Canon

Church law, or canon, did not allow the clergy to shed blood, a regulation that one might assume was common knowledge among medieval bishops. Yet the *Song of Roland*, which describes the military actions of Charlemagne's rear guard at Roncesvalles, places Bishop Turpin at Roland's side killing Saracens with the swordlike precision of a helicopter blade. Though the real battle occurred in 778, the earliest written version, embellished with the attributes of Christian chivalry, dates from the twelfth century. Both dates fall within the period known as the Age of Faith.

William the Conqueror's half-brother, Odo, Bishop of Bayeux and also Earl of Kent, noticed that the Latin verb in the canon forbidding the clerical shedding of blood was *to cut*. And so, the Bishop of Bayeux rode forth into battle carrying a mace, adhering, not to the spirit of the law, but rather to the letter of the law, by employing a blunt instrument that did not cut.

## Avoiding Blood Feuds

In primitive Germanic and Nordic societies, most laws were unwritten and each dispute was decided by the community graybeards. The need to ward off blood feuds was crucial, because otherwise the unending feuds would destroy the security of tribal structure, and there was not always a Beowulf present to thwart outside threats. The *wergeld* was merely a method that dictated some form of payment for a tort offense against another member of the community. Specific values were assigned on the basis of both the seriousness of the offense and the stature or age of the victim. Offenses included what we call murder and manslaughter, in addition to personal injury and property damage.

To cause the death of an aged man or of a woman well beyond childbearing years demanded a smaller payment than did causing the death of persons in their prime, and wounding or cutting off bodily members demanded a smaller sum still. The *wergeld* system prevented anyone from serving as their own judge or from engaging in an act of vengeance that might lead to a destructive chain reaction.

## Western and Eastern Medical Practice

The Muslims of the Near East were very conscious of the scientific and medical knowledge that was part of the Greek heritage. They translated, borrowed, and adapted from these materials as rationally suited their needs. The Crusades brought Western and Eastern customs into both conflict and contrast, a situation painfully revealed in a record left by a Syrian physician named Thabit. Thabit was brought two patients, a knight with a serious abscess in his leg and a woman running a high fever. He applied a cataplasm to cause the abscess to drain, with positive signs of healing. He prescribed a revision of diet for the woman and successfully lowered her temperature.

At this point, however, a Frankish (crusader) doctor arrived and asserted that the infidel physician certainly could not cure these people, and immediately asked the knight whether he wished to remain alive with a single leg or die with two. Of course the patient preferred life with one leg over death, and thus the Frankish doctor summoned a knight with a sharp axe and ordered him to remove the leg with a single blow. The first blow was unsuccessful and the knight was forced to strike again. However, he did not hit the same spot, instead shattering the bone, and the patient expired.

As to the treatment of the feverish woman, the Frankish doctor's examination uncovered the presence of a devil in her head, and he demanded that her head be shaved immediately. She returned to her former diet of heavily spiced foods, her fever grew worse, and the doctor then prescribed even stronger treatments. Using a razor, he carved into her scalp the shape of a cross, scraping the lines of the cross until he reached the bone. Then he rubbed the skull with salt to expel the devil that had obviously entered the patient's head. The woman also died as a result of this doctor's treatment.

# Medieval Legal Procedures

Dating from Roman times as *ius primae noctis* and known to manorial and feudal law by the French term *droit de seigneur*, the lord of a manor in some European regions could enjoy "right of first night" with the bride of a newly married serf. The serf then redeemed his wife by the payment of a customary fee. While the first night practice itself fell into disuse by the High Middle Ages, the custom of the fee payment survived in Bavaria until the eighteenth century.

Feudal law reflected a special reverence for landed property and for all that God had provided to aid in land use. In his *Medieval Village*, G. G. Coulton tells of a German code that protected trees used as supports for the dykes built to prevent flooding of tilled fields. Should one remove the bark from such a tree the prescribed punishment was to have "his belly ripped up, and his bowels shall be taken out and wound around the harm he has done."

Trial by combat survived in practice until the thirteenth century and, in theory, for several centuries after that. Pope Innocent III (1198–1216) and the Fourth Lateran Council forbade trials by combat in 1216, and shortly afterward the rulers of most lands began to enforce prohibitions against this formula for resolving civil or criminal disputes. H. C. Lea, in his *Superstition and Force*, supplies one of the more startling examples of trial by combat, which we must understand was a test of honesty—God sided with the innocent party by giving a sign—and which also had the collateral benefit of resolution, to prevent the blood feud.

In 1127, a knight named Guy was accused by another knight, Hermann, as having been an accomplice in the assassination of Charles the Good of Flanders; when Guy denied the charges, Hermann demanded proof of his innocence by judicial combat. The two fought for hours and, according to a line from an off-color limerick, tore up trees, shrubs, and flowers. Eventually they were both without horse and weapon and hence resorted to wrestling. In the ferocity of the fight Hermann tore Guy's testicles from his body, thus proving his charge. God had given a sign, and Guy quickly died.

Even branding was known to medieval law, and as a punishment for a variety of crimes it lasted into the seventeenth century.

Brands were a painful and lasting advertisement of what crimes lay in an individual's past. For perjury and blasphemy piercing the tongue with a shaft of hot iron was a common punishment, while in England one might find a scar on a convict's forehead that was made up of the letters S.O.S.—sewer of sedition.

## Anglo-Saxon Legal Processes

Rather than substantive, Anglo-Saxon law was essentially procedural in character. A trial for tort action did not include either a jury or eyewitness testimony, a reflection of the belief that humans are weak and basically prone to evil, and hence will lie. Thus, decisions rested with God and very strict and formal steps were taken during which God would give a sign to indicate which was the guilty party. The following case is fictionalized but the procedure is historically accurate.

One day, Esgar swings his sword at a tree branch and accidentally cuts off Aethelstan's thumb. Charged with the act and brought by his guarantors before the village court, Esgar claims Aethelstan walked into the sword and hence no tort should be charged. Each must now deliver a formally structured oath attesting to their claim, but it is not the content of the oaths that is most important. Rather, it is essential that the oath be delivered perfectly: There must be no pauses, no tripping over a word, and nothing left out. If either fails, God has given a sign and judgment is awarded to the other. Should no sign be forthcoming, oath helpers of equal numbers will follow the same procedure and attest to the quality of an oath (compurgation), but not to any facts in the case. If Aethelstan ultimately loses, he will in the future be considered a perjurer with a less valuable oath. If Esgar loses, then he will be the perjurer, will pay the value of the lost thumb, and will surrender to the king the diadem of his sword, since it has shed blood for an unacceptable reason.

Now, let us complicate the matter. At some future date Esgar, already a known perjurer, is the only one present with another party and said party is killed by the blow of a sword. Many know they were together but there are no witnesses to the act. Esgar's denial of involvement is of no significance and he will be ordered to undergo an ordeal so that God may decide his guilt or innocence. Among several common ordeals—including being thrown into a river with both arms and legs bound by rope (pure water will reject the guilty and accept the innocent), successfully swallowing a large ball of dough without choking, carrying a hot iron on the hands for a prescribed distance—the ordeal of scalding water is chosen. Esgar's arm is plunged up to the elbow into a caldron of boiling water, so that he receives a severe burn. The burn is then wrapped in cloth blessed by the local priest. After a specific number of days the arm is unwrapped and examined. If the burn shows all indications of normal and rapid healing God has spoken in Esgar's favor, but if it is still blistered and has festered, Esgar is off to the hangman's noose.

Let us add but one more twist to this fictional case with the simplest of events. Esgar jabs his sword into a table, but does so insecurely, and while he and Aethelstan are eating the sword falls over and severs the latter's toe. If there is no dispute and Esgar concedes all, the verdict will be logical in Anglo-Saxon law: Esgar is responsible for damages caused by his property, in the same fashion that a resident of San Francisco would be responsible if the brakes of his or her parked car suddenly failed and the car crashed into Ghirardelli Square. Esgar pays the damages, and, of course, loses his sword as a diadem.

## Religious Power in Northern France

All students of the Middle Ages are particularly indebted to the many volumes written or edited by G. G. Coulton on the life, work, beliefs, and practices of medieval people. Among his preserved stories about the people of northern France, within the ranks of the simple and the unlettered, one of the most charming is the tale of a jackdaw (large crow) who resided in the trees surrounding a monastery in Reims. The story involves the power of the bishop to excommunicate and thereby withhold God's blessings.

The abbot (or superior) of a local monastery, who lived a fine life that was quite above acceptable standards, when washing his hands one day for an obviously sumptuous meal, removed his rings, which were of great value, and placed them beside the washbasin. Later the valuable items were gone. A careful search of all areas of the buildings and grounds, and a thorough inter-rogation of all the brethren and staff, turned up no clues. The abbot consulted the local bishop and the head of the diocese and all agreed it was obviously an "inside job." So the bishop excom-municated (withheld all blessings of the sacraments) the guilty party, whoever it might be.

As days turned into weeks with no evidence of the abbot's rings, the clergy and staff of the monastery noted that the pet jackdaw who lived in a tree near the kitchen was losing his feathers. He looked ill and weak, and was without his usual zest and appetite. Most believed him to be on the road to death. However, one of the monks climbed a tree where the jackdaw kept a nest, and there, as he had suspected, the monk found the abbot's rings. He promptly returned the rings to his gracious master, who asked that the bishop lift the excommunication. In the weeks that followed it was noted by all of the monastery's inhabitants how the jackdaw regained his previous vitality and appetite, moved about swiftly, and enjoyed a new and healthy growth of feathers. No one will ever know how many of France's faithful, through several generations, heard and repeated this story during the eleventh and twelfth centuries.

# An Ambassador at the Byzantine Court

In 963 Otto I (king of Germany from 912 to 973) sent Bishop Liutprand of Cremona to the imperial court of Constantinople to arrange a marriage between Byzantine Princess Theophano and the future Otto II. Arrangements were frustrated largely owing to the attitudes of Byzantine Emperor Nicephorus II Phocas. Liutprand was a cultured Italian prelate who has left us a quite unfavorable evaluation of the Byzantine emperor and his court.

The bishop described the reception, quarters, and living condi-tions for his mission as simply miserable. No transportation was provided for long walks, and he likened the wine to an undrinkable mixture of "pitch, resin and plaster." The water was unsafe and could not be drunk at all.

Finally, on the fourth day of his visit, Liutprand was ushered to the Crown Palace and into the presence of Emperor Nicephorus. He has left the following description of the emperor: "A monstrosity of a man, a dwarf, fat-headed and with tiny mole eyes; disfigured by a short, broad, thick beard half going gray; disgraced by a neck scarcely an inch long; pig-like by reason of the big close bristles on his head; in color an Ethiopian and, as the poet says, 'you would not like to meet him in the dark'; a big belly, a lean posterior, very long in the hip considering his short stature, small legs, fair sized heels and feet; dressed in a robe made of fine linen, but old, foul smelling and discolored by age; shod with Sicyonian slippers; bold of tongue, a fox by nature, in perjury and falsehood a Ulysses."

## Wooden Tax Receipts in England

By the reign of England's Henry I (1100–1135), who was known as Beauclerc owing to the efficiency of his administration, collecting funds owed to the king had become more precise. At Easter and Michaelmas (September 29) the royal treasurer and judiciary sat before members of the Curia Regis at a table covered by a check-ered cloth. Amounts due or paid were computed by tallies, or counters, using the squares of cloth. When all was accounted for, the board was cleared and a receipt prepared in "duplicate." This receipt was a wooden tally (or paddle) that had a hole in one end, so it could be "filed," and identical notches of various depths carved on each side. The depth of each notch indicated the amount paid by the sheriff, who was discouraged from carving the notches deeper because of the state's identical copy of his receipt.

Thus doubly carved, the paddle was split vertically down the middle; one half went to the sheriff and the other was retained by the Treasury as a permanent record. The half retained by the Treasury would be strung on string or wire, much like the large beads once used to keep score overhead in a poolroom. These wooden receipts remained as a part of medieval financial history until a fire destroyed the Parliament buildings in 1834.

## Misconceptions of Magna Carta

Among several interesting facts regarding the great constitutional document Magna Carta is that King John never signed it. John probably could not even write, but in any event, the great seal was affixed to signify acceptance, according to standard procedure. It is a common error to refer to the "signing" of Magna Carta; in fact, Queen Elizabeth II did so in a dedication ceremony at Runnymede in 1965.

It is also known that Magna Carta was not established as a list of liberties, but rather as a treaty between the great barons of the realm and King John, so as to guarantee their baronial and feudal rights. The so-called rights for all Englishmen would be read into the document later by angry commoners or won by soldiers like Oliver Cromwell. However, the most significant feature of Magna Carta is that three of its more than sixty articles deal with a nonfeudal class of individuals—merchants—and their needs. This was exactly the class of persons whose success spelled doom for the political-economic dominance of the document's very authors, because it was the merchant class that provided the king with the funds to hire his own army, so long as he granted charters to their towns and their trades.

## Some Medieval Peters Earn Their Names

Peter Comester (c. 1100–1180), from the 1140s until his death, served in several responsible positions that included dean of the cathedral at Troyes, chancellor of the cathedral school at Paris, and instructor in theology at the same location. He wrote a *Scholastic History*, many commentaries on the Bible and the writings of great church scholars, and contributed in a general way to the theological milieu of twelfth-century Paris. Perhaps his most unusual and interesting trait is his name, which, according to tradition, derived from his insatiable appetite and extreme obesity. Hence he is known as Peter Comester, which means "Peter the eater" in Latin.

Also an ecclesiastic, but certainly not a scholar, was Peter the Hermit (c. 1050–1115) who, though dubbed Peter the Little by contemporaries owing to his small stature, is known to history as the Hermit. This label arose from his common practice of wearing a hermit's cloak, which fit well the style and purpose of one who went barefoot in all seasons, never bathed, abstained from meat and bread, and confined himself to an almost exclusive diet of fish and wine. He is best known to history for preaching on the need for a crusade to the Holy Land among the rabble of France and the Rhineland, and also for leading a horde of Europe's unwashed through Hungary to Constantinople, just prior to the First Crusade (1096). Emperor Alexius Comnenus, not wishing to have such a scavenging throng within his territories, provided transportation for them to Asia Minor, where they were quickly routed by a Muslim army. Peter the Hermit survived to later disgrace himself (by fleeing instead of fighting) during the siege of Antioch by Bohemond I of Taranto, and ultimately returned to Belgium, where he died in a monastery near Huy. It is also of interest that his chief cohort in preaching and leading the crusade was known as Walter the Penniless (in French Gautier sans Avoir).

# Student Life and Friction with Local Residents

In his study *Universities of Europe During the Middle Ages*, Professor Hastings Rashdall quotes generously from the comments of a monk named Jacques de Vitry (c. 1230) and from the monk's descriptions of students studying in Paris. For essentially academic activities, these students were confined to the island surrounding the cathedral of Notre Dame, and later were allowed to expand to the area on the left bank of the Seine. Since that time this section of the left bank has been known as the Latin Quarter, owing to the prescription that students speak Latin outside the classroom as well as in.

According to the monk, most students were loose in moral conduct and did not consider excessive fornication to be sinful, and it was not unusual for students to attend lectures on the second floor of a structure whose first floor was a brothel. As de Vitry put it, "Debates of philosophers could be heard with the quarrels of courtesans and pimps." Students of various nationalities came to see each other according to stereotypes that carried something of the modern disreputable ring associated with the Texas Aggie jokes. According to these stereotypes, the English were heavy drinkers and had tails, the French were proud and "effeminate," the Germans were given to "blustering" when drunk, and the Flemish were fat and greedy.

Because of his status, which gave him the ecclesiastical immunities of a cleric, the student was exempt from many forms of taxation, military service, and prosecution in secular courts. This led of course to many violent struggles between town and gown, and a general hostility toward students among other town residents. As a matter of fact the development of Cambridge University is attributed to acts of violence at Oxford. It began when a woman was killed by an Oxford student in 1209, to which townspeople responded by raiding a student residence hall and hanging several students. In protest of this lynching, according to Matthew Paris, 3,000 students and many masters left en masse and set up classes near the bridge on the Cam River. Subsequent endorsements for separate colleges led to the fine university we find there today.

## Louis IX, the Royal Saint

What actions, conduct, or accomplishments qualified a monarch to be canonized by the Universal Church, an accolade that makes any person a member of one of the most exclusive fraternities in recorded history? Eighteen campaigns to firmly establish Christianity among the Saxons and the famous expedition against the Muslims of Spain (celebrated in the *Song of Roland*) did not win such holy distinction for Charlemagne. England's Edward the Confessor did not make it, nor did his most Catholic majesty Philip II of Spain, who spent billions (by modern standards) on armies, navies, expeditions, and missionaries to reclaim Europe for the true faith and even fashioned his own palace (Escorial) on the plan of the gridiron on which Saint Lawrence died a martyr.

So we must ask what kind of man was Louis IX (1226–1270), a contemporary of Henry III of England and Frederick II of Germany and Italy, who lived while the memory and the brothers of the order of Saint Francis of Assisi spread throughout western Europe?

Consider the following list, largely based upon the writings of Louis IX's aide and court historian, Jean de Joinville:

1. Son of the strong-willed and sincerely religious Blanche of Castille, who was his official regent for much of his reign, Louis

was hurried into marriage without the usual wenching, and became a model husband and parent who took a personal role in the education of his 11 children. He lived a simple life free of luxury and established a reputation for good and just government tempered with charity.

2. When a nobleman within royal jurisdiction hanged two Flemish students for killing rabbits on his estate, King Louis threatened the nobleman with a similar fate, then had him temporarily imprisoned and upon the nobleman's release imposed a penance that included the construction of three chapels, the donation of the forest location of the crime to an abbey, the forfeiture of the nobleman's own hunting privileges, a three-year term of service in the Holy Land, and the payment of a hefty fine. Throughout the realm, Louis improved and expanded the quality and availability of sound justice.

3. On the international scene, he built such a reputation for strength tempered with honesty, fairness, and honor that he alone among contemporaries was a peacemaker and highly regarded arbiter of disputes or wars. William of Chartres said, "Men feared him because they knew that he was just." Hence, there was no war against the Christian states. And Joinville said that "on no day of my life did I ever hear him speak evil of anyone."

4. When captured during his first crusade to North Africa, Louis was released and trusted to pay the remaining 10,000 livres (approximately $2 million) of his ransom. He paid the remainder against the advice of his counselors.

5. The king dispensed justice while sitting under a tree in the forest near Vincennes. In religious ceremonies, he washed the feet of the poor and the blind without their knowledge of his identity. He also tortured his own flesh and often wore a haircloth shirt under the robes of a pilgrim.

6. He shared his personal wealth with the poor and with the new Franciscan and Dominican mendicants. Each day he heard two masses, recited his prayers five times, said 50 Ave Marias before retiring, and rose at midnight to join the priests at matins in chapel. He even abstained from marital intercourse during Advent and Lent, and was once told by a lady that he seemed more equipped to be king of all monastic orders than of a nation.

7. He appreciated the more popular and common religious practices of his times, a fact evidenced by his purchase from agents in the Holy Land of a nail that had pierced the Saviour, the crown of

thorns worn by Jesus during the Passion, and a piece of the true cross. To house these and other holy items obtained in his travels and crusades, he constructed Sainte Chapelle in Paris, on an island in the Seine.

8. Not unlike Saint Francis, the rigors and austerities of his life of devotion rendered Louis IX old and weak before his time. Yet despite his aging, which was coupled with malaria and anemia, he prepared and launched a second crusade in 1270, this time to Tunisia. Shortly after his arrival, he died of what the chroniclers politely called in French *le peste*. Though the first translation is "plague," the historian knows it here to mean dysentery. Louis was canonized in 1297, and all French historians agree that he was the most Christian king of the Middle Ages.

## The Murder of Saint Thomas Becket

By the late twelfth century the most important religious shrine in England was the tomb of Saint Thomas Becket at Canterbury Cathedral. Most are familiar with the conflict between Becket and King Henry II, who were boozing and wenching buddies. These great friends became enemies during a serious struggle that came after Henry had elevated Becket from chancellor to Archbishop of Canterbury, primate of all England. Becket eventually met his death at the hands of Henry's knights, supposedly on the high altar in 1170. Pope Alexander III (1159–1181) canonized Becket within two years after his death, and Henry performed penance and accepted public humiliation for the deed.

Any constitutional historian who examines the political-religious conflict between the two parties would, contrary to popular belief and the convenience of Hollywood film-makers, name Becket the true heavy, not Henry II.

Justification for such a position is easy to assemble:

1. The Church was the richest institution in all England, and the lands administered by its hierarchy were part of the military and economic underpinnings of the Crown. Henry II at least needed the same share in selecting the church hierarchy as had been agreed upon by Henry I in 1107—the cathedral chapter elected a bishop in the king's presence, the nominee paid homage to the Crown for the lands and properties that accompanied the office,

and then the nominee was anointed with symbols of office by superior clergymen or by the pope. There was probably not a clergyman of significance in England who did not find this arrangement a fair and proper compromise, except Becket, the newly "reborn" archbishop.

2. Henry II was a man of sound juridical outlook, and he liked an orderly realm. The chaotic civil strife between his mother Matilda and Stephen of Blois that preceded his reign left much to be done by the tools for which he is so well known to historians—assizes, writs, juries. Becket took issue with one of these legal compromises (found in the *Constitutions of Clarendon*, which contains the reforms proposed by Henry II) that specifically sought to restore order, civility, and security. This compromise applied to the following situation: An armed robber is apprehended plying his trade on a royal highway. He claims to be a clergyman, and hence immune to the authority of royal courts. He pleads "benefit of clergy," which means that his case must be heard and the punishment—often some form of penance—decided by the church courts. Therefore, the case is prosecuted according to church canon, not civil law. The compromise sought by the *Constitutions* provided for the accused's status as a clergyman—ability to read Latin, etc.—to be determined by a royal court. If the royal court determines that the robber is in fact a clergyman, he is first charged with the crime by the royal court, then released to the church courts to be tried. If the accused is proven guilty, he is returned to the royal courts for sentencing. Through this compromise Henry attempted to deal with the problem of "criminous clerks." Becket alone, of all consequential English clergy and lawyers, opposed this arrangement. All others felt it conformed with the traditions and practices of English polity since the time of William the Conqueror (d. 1087).

3. Finally, in the heat of their dispute, Becket went into self-imposed exile in English royal lands across the Channel, to pray and meditate; Henry sought him out. In a one-on-one conference, Becket gave Henry clear reason to believe that the future would bring a positive resolution of their conflicts. He then returned to England, leaving Henry on the Continent. Once in England, however, the archbishop decreed that all clergy who conformed to the *Constitutions* and/or who participated in the coronation of Henry's heir would be excommunicated. Henry was at first dumbfounded, but then became furious. In the company of a group of armed knights, Henry vented his anger: "What, shall a man who has eaten my bread . . . insult the king and all the

kingdom, and not one of the lazy servants whom I nourish at my table does me right for such an affront?" Four knights did right by their king, murdering Becket in December of 1170, and by 1172 Thomas Becket was made a saint.

# Bohemond I Seizes Antioch

The contingent of crusaders that marched across southern Asia Minor (modern Turkey) in 1097 was soon halted by the fortifications of Antioch. Among the several leaders of the First Crusade, by far the most daring and adventurous, and certainly the least loyal to his vows of allegiance to the Byzantine emperor at Constantinople, was Bohemond I of Taranto, one of the land-hungry sons of Robert Guiscard. The siege of Antioch dragged on into 1098, seriously depleting the resources and supplies of both defenders and attackers. Finally, Bohemond was able to bribe a Muslim defender to open one of the gates of the walled city at an appointed hour. He then offered a bargain to his fellow commanders in the competitive spirit and gamesmanship of chivalry—whichever of them was first to successfully breach the walls and gain entry should be the new governor of the city. Antioch fell; Bohemond became the new ruler and reneged on his oath to restore all conquered properties to the Byzantine emperor. Instead, he sent to Emperor Alexius I Comnenus (1081–1118) a cargo of noses and thumbs.

# Religious Power on the First Crusade

Another story about Antioch, for which we are essentially indebted to chroniclers such as Raimond of Agiles and Fulcher of Chartres, involves the counterattack of Muslim forces after Bohemond I became ruler. Desperation gripped the beleaguered crusaders until the supposed discovery of the Holy Lance (the spear that had pierced the side of the dying Jesus). Raimond of Agiles tells us that two piles of dry olive branches—each pile measuring thirteen feet in length and four in height, with but one foot between them—were lighted and burned fiercely. Then, after prayers and ceremonial blessings, dressed only in his tunic but

with the Holy Lance in hand, Peter Bartholomew, who supposedly had discovered the lance, was chosen to march into the flames.
He paused briefly in the center and emerged without hint of injury
to himself or the lance, confirming the qualities of the lance.
Subsequently the crusaders, inspired by what they considered a
symbol of divine favor, rallied to defeat the infidel forces and end
the siege of Antioch. They then continued their march toward the
holy city of Jerusalem.

## Two Conquests of Jerusalem

For the brutal and bloody conquest of Jerusalem we have two
eyewitness accounts, one by Raimond of Agiles and another by
William of Tyre, in his *History of Deeds Done Beyond the Sea.* These
accounts are very similar in nearly all specifics of the carnage,
looting, rape, and pillage, and also in their portrayal of the
ultimate scene when refugees crowded into the sacred temple.
Both describe the quantity of blood as a river that drenched even
the attackers—a kind of sea of floating body parts. In broad
contrast, nearly a century later (1187) we have an entirely different
story, when Jerusalem was successfully conquered by the revived
and powerful Muslim armies of Saladin. In this battle there was
no slaughter. Rich Christians were freed after payment of ransom.
Saladin even released 3,000 without ransom and later liberated all
the aged and legitimate pilgrims. Christians who remained in
Jerusalem under Muslim rule were required to pay a modest poll
tax and were refused the right to bear arms.

## The Second Crusade and
## Eleanor of Aquitaine

The extremely devout Louis VII (1137–1180) of France was one of
the two royal participants in the Second Crusade (1146–1148), a
venture that proved disastrous for the Christian forces of both
France and Germany. Louis's queen, the famous and often
troublesome Eleanor of Aquitaine, accompanied him along with
the countesses of Flanders and Toulouse. Eastern Christian
leaders were amused by the willingness of the Frankish forces to

bring women and the consequent heavy trunks and boxes of apparel and cosmetics. It seems evident that there must have been some substance to rumors regarding the time Eleanor spent in festive activities with her entourage of troubadours and musicians. So far and so long did such rumors persist that one (false, of course) had Eleanor romantically involved with the Muslim leader Saladin, who at the time of the Second Crusade would have been a small boy as yet unknown to recorded history. No doubt such views of Eleanor's temperament were encouraged by reports that she referred to her husband as "that monk."

## The Third Crusade, a Crusade of Kings

It is the Third Crusade (1189–1192) that has received the most attention from Hollywood film producers, probably because it was led by three strong and noteworthy monarchs, one of whom was the famous Richard the Lion-Hearted. Rather than a myth or legend, Richard was the genuine article. English historian Austin Lane-Poole, after careful evaluation of various chronicles, assures us that Richard was an excellent commander, who often engaged in glorious and skillful personal combat, never relented when exposed to physical danger, and even won the respect and admiration of Saladin himself for his chivalrous prowess. When Richard became ill and was racked by fever during the Third Crusade, Saladin sent him fresh foods, medicine, and doctors. It is also true that Richard was captured by the duke of Austria, imprisoned for ransom, ultimately released, and then returned to the crusading cause. He was certainly blessed with good fortune, for despite his many campaigns he did not die by the sword, and he enjoyed a stable government, large tax revenues, and loyalty from his subjects (brother John excepted) even though he only spent a total of ten months in England during his ten-year reign.

## The Children's Crusade

In 1212 a German youth now known only as Nicholas proclaimed that God had commissioned him to lead a crusade of children to the Holy Land (although not numbered, this followed the scandalous Fourth Crusade). Both clergy and laymen condemned his plan and tried to halt enthusiasm that rose on his behalf.

Eventually thousands of youths (including some girls dressed as boys) joined Nicholas. The group left from Cologne, followed the Rhine valley, crossed the Alps, braved weather, thieves, wolves, and death, and arrived minus the fallen at Genoa. The Italians laughed at them, Pope Innocent III told them to return to their homes, and disillusionment caused the youths to scatter in several directions.

In France, during the same year, a 12-year-old shepherd named Stephen reported to King Philip Augustus that Jesus had appeared to him as he tended his flocks; the Lord had instructed him to lead a children's crusade to Palestine. The king ordered Stephen to return home, possibly affected by the memory of his own illness during the Third Crusade. Nevertheless, some 20,000 youngsters rallied to Stephen's banner and made their way across France to the port of Marseilles, where Stephen had promised them that the sea would divide as it had for Moses and permit the march to the Holy Land. But the miracle failed to unfold. Two ship owners agreed to transport the group free of charge and soon left with seven ships packed with hymn-singing youths. Two ships were wrecked near Sardinia without survivors, while the children on board the other five were deposited at either Egypt or Tunisia and sold into slavery. The ship owners were hanged on the orders of Frederick II, the Holy Roman Emperor.

## Saint Francis of Assisi, History's Favorite Friar

There is a mural on the wall of the upper great church at Assisi. Attributed to Giotto, it depicts the dream of Pope Innocent III (1198–1216) in which the collapsing walls of the papal cathedral, the church of Saint John Lateran, are the central feature. According to the story, Pope Innocent had chosen not to recognize Francis of Assisi and his devoted followers owing to the severity of their self-punishment and austerities performed in the service of God. Then, the very night after his refusal, the pope experienced a fitful dream in which, while he lay helpless on his bed, he and his cathedral were preserved by the strength of a simple barefoot man in peasants' clothing. Saint Bonaventure assures us that Innocent's devotion to Francis was inspired by this incident.

Even most modern historians choose not to argue the validity of the many stories that surround the devoted but physically tortuous life of Francis of Assisi. The life of this simple friar inspired works by some of the greatest artists and scholars (for example, Giotto and Dante) and furnished the substance for miracle plays that formed the roots of modern drama. There is probably no more appealing saint in all of Christian history, and a case can be made for the claim that, after he had fully converted and become a servant of Jesus, no figure more Christlike ever walked the earth.

The stories tell of a man who preached to birds that ceased singing and sat at his feet while he advised them to always be grateful to God for their carefree life. He would give his own simple rags to shivering beggars, ignore his own nutritional needs to provide for others, carry on in indifference to his own pain and fever, which led to the ultimate destruction of his health, and criticize wealth and laxity while working for the poor, weak, and sick (lepers). He had all the spiritual energy of what might best be described as a "God-intoxicated" man. Though Saint Francis is not the only figure who could be described this way, in his case this spiritual intoxication always brought positive results for all humanity. He once forced a devoted follower, Brother Barbaro, to eat a lump of ass's dung for having spoken evil of another, and held the loyalty of his flock by his own examples of rectitude and bravery. He attempted to convert the sultan of Egypt by going alone into the enemy Muslim camp, preaching, and winning respect as a man of God. Finally, there is little argument with the most startling of the Saint Francis stories. Contemporary reports reveal that in the closing hours of his life the saint suffered bleeding in the same locations as that experienced by Jesus in his crucifixion. Francis was canonized less than three years after his death.

# A King Called Wonder of the World

As Hohenstaufen heir, Frederick II became the successor to the throne of the Holy Roman Empire in 1198, at the age of four. His early education and training came under the guardianship of Pope Innocent III; in 1212 he declared his majority. Frederick established his royal courts in Aachen and Foggia (he preferred south Italy) and, over the years until his death in 1250, earned one of the most memorable reputations of all medieval monarchs. Few equaled his versatility in intellect, politics, or statecraft, and much of his record anticipates the view of man that is usually considered a legacy of the Renaissance. Some examples of this are

1. He was the best administrator of the century among European royalty, contributing to improved government and general prosperity in every region under his authority. Frederick was the first ruler since Justinian (525–565) to systematically codify law, with the aid of legal scholars.

2. He was excommunicated several times by several popes, and spent much of his adult life under a papal ban. The first occasion came when war delayed his departure for the Holy Land for the crusade he had vowed to lead, and the second when illness caused further delay. After the ban had been lifted upon his arrival in the Near East, he was again excommunicated for negotiating with infidels, despite the fact that by treaty he gained more in territory and concessions for the Roman Church than others had through conquest.

3. During his youth in southern Italy and Sicily, Frederick came into contact with Jews, Muslims, and Greek Christians. His ability to speak Arabic was one of the keys to his successes in the Holy Land. This varied cultural background also developed in him a curious, alert mind and a cosmopolitan approach to problems and events.

In his study of Frederick II, historian E. Kantorowicz claims that the emperor spoke more than a half-dozen languages and presided over a royal court at Foggia consisting of mistresses, slaves, acrobats, dancers, and a menagerie of exotic animals that included leopards, lynxes, lions, and apes. Next to hunting, he delighted in sophisticated conversation that both demonstrated and enhanced his broad learning and curious mind. Tradition says that he experimented with small children unexposed to human voices to see if they would mature to speak the oldest tongue (Hebrew), the language of their natural parents, or that of the region where they were raised. In addition to attempting to hatch ostrich eggs in the warm Apulian sun (he knew it could be done with sand in Africa), he supposedly had a newly deceased corpse encased in a wine vat and observed around the clock to see if the soul could be detected upon its departure from the flesh. His learning and cultural tolerance led to an array of false charges that he was an atheist (made by astrologers at the royal court), a Jew, and even a Muslim. He never tolerated heresy within Christianity, however, which was probably the only area where he and the various popes saw eye to eye.

# What To Do with the Ashes of a Burned Heretic

The Universal Church of the Middle Ages held that the writings of the Patristic Fathers (for example, Saint Augustine of Hippo), official pronouncements of popes and ecumenical councils (for example, the Nicene Creed and the doctrine of the Trinity), and church canon were equal to Holy Scripture in truth and righteousness. Open challenge to or preaching against these elements was seen as challenging or preaching against God, not the Church, and was hence to be punished. If convicted of such crimes by the proper ecclesiastical judicial body, a heretic was to be punished by burning if he or she both persisted in preaching falsehoods and refused to recant. The ashes of heretics were thrown into a swift river lest any of his or her followers seek to employ them as the instructional tools of martyrdom.

A fine example of such a sequence of events is the case of Arnold of Brescia (d. 1155), a monk who had studied under Abelard and who practiced the severest austerities on his body. Though generally orthodox in theological matters, Arnold of Brescia openly attacked the wealth of the clergy and the Church, and demanded a return to apostolic poverty and simplicity. He went too far, however, when he charged that sinful clergy could not truly administer the sacraments: That is, he believed that the Holy Spirit would not come to the aid of any Christian who received the sacraments from a priest who was in a state of sin. The charge was a threat to the wealth and power of the clergy, and also represented the judgment of a simple monk rather than that of a bishop, pope, or council.

With the aid of popular support and the rescission of the orders of previous popes to be silent, Arnold seized control of the city of

Rome, drove out the current pope (Eugenius III), and presided over a restored Roman Republic for ten years. Finally, when Holy Roman Emperor Frederick Barbarossa led an army to Rome in 1155, he restored the pope (by then Pope Adrian IV—Nicholas Breakspear—the only English pope in all of history) to his residences and had Arnold apprehended and hanged for his resistance to imperial authority. Afterward, Arnold's remains were burned and his ashes thrown into the Tiber River, according to proper procedure.

In 1415, John Hus spoke before the gathered clergy of the Council of Constance, defending propositions regarding clerical sin and wealth that were similar to the charges made by Arnold of Brescia. Nullifying his safe-conduct guarantee from Emperor Sigismund, the council condemned him to death and his ashes were likewise dispersed. The same council also condemned John Wycliffe (d. 1384) for his teachings in England and ordered his bones exhumed, burned, and thrown into a river. The same procedure was followed after Joan of Arc was burned in the market square of Rouen in 1431.

# Brutal Retribution by Papal Authority

Much in the same fashion and with similar criticisms as those launched by Arnold of Brescia (burned in Rome in 1155), Dolcino of Novara and his sister Margherita, in 1303, attacked both the Church and the upper clergy for their wealth and corruption. Dolcino charged that since the fourth century all popes except Celestine V (who died after a few months' tenure in 1294) had been unfaithful to Jesus, that the work of saints Francis and Dominic had failed, and that popes now presided over what he termed the harlot of the Apocalypse. Forming a new fraternity called the Apostolic Brethren of Parma, Dolcino, his sister, and their followers rejected the authority of popes, vowed chastity, and verbally attacked Church wealth. Ordered to appear before a tribunal of the Inquisition, they refused, armed themselves, and retreated to defensible positions in the Piedmontese Alps. The Inquisition sent an army against them, and after several bloody battles the Brethren were reduced to eating grass, rats, and dogs. Eventually their bastion was overtaken, and thousands were made prisoner. Many were burned for heresy, including Dolcino's loyal sister Margherita, who refused to recant even as the flames rose about her. In his study of the Inquisition, H. C. Lea tells us that Dolcino and his closest confederate were mounted on a cart and paraded through the city of Vercelli, while their flesh was torn away bit by bit with hot pincers and then all their limbs were torn from their bodies.

## Abelard's Love, Castration, and Remembrance

No student of the cultural life of twelfth-century France will find a scholar, philosopher, teacher, or personality whose career was more striking than that of the Breton who came to join the theological debates in and around Paris. This was Peter Abelard (d. 1142), popular with students and open-minded debaters and abhorred by Bernard of Clairvaux, the "Hound of the Heretics." But apart from the world of ideas, philosophy, and the contentious harangues of academic discussion, Abelard is one of the most tragic figures in history—a fact owing to the personal and romantic developments in his life. Indeed, the tale of his personal misfortune reads like a soap opera. All the essential details are known because Abelard himself left a reasonably complete description in his *Historia Calamitation.*

Fulbert, a cathedral canon, had a lovely niece named Heloise whose convent training had, by age 16, provided her with solid knowledge of Latin and French and had also earned the special admiration of her uncle. Abelard was invited to live with Fulbert and his niece, and served as Heloise's tutor. What started as mere physical attraction between teacher and student soon grew into "a tenderness surpassing in sweetness the most fragrant balm."

Soon Heloise was with child, upon which Abelard arranged for her to live with a sister in Brittany and, having revealed all to Fulbert, agreed to marry the young woman if Fulbert would concur in keeping the marriage a secret. That way Heloise would be matrimonially sanctified while Abelard's vows were protected and his prominent role in higher scholastic education secured as well. Heloise had such strong respect for Abelard and his career, however, that she temporarily refused marriage and contemplated following canon prescriptions by surrendering the child to a foundling home and becoming a nun. She did not wish, according to Abelard's own words, to rob from philosophy and the Church "so shining a light." After long pleading she surrendered to the marriage contract, but only when she was given the firm guarantee that all would remain a secret.

The two loved ones lived apart, visiting clandestinely, and everything might have worked out had Fulbert not had a change of heart, revealed the facts, and openly chastised his niece. Heloise lied and denied the marriage, but Abelard took swift action and, against her will, had her ensconced in a convent at Argenteuil so she might live the life of a nun. Fully angered (and obviously not understanding the true tenderness of the relationship), Fulbert, in the words of Abelard, "laid a plot against me. . . . I was asleep in a secret room of my lodgings, they broke in . . . they had vengeance upon me with a most cruel and painful punishment . . . for they cut off those parts of my body whereby I had done that which was the cause of their sorrow."

Because we have both the account of Abelard and the letters he shared with Heloise we enjoy a very detailed picture of their relationship. It seems that each was completely devoted to the other, a rare situation in most relationships. This bittersweet love story was retold by Jean-Jacques Rousseau in his epistolary novel *Julie, or the New Heloise* (published 1761), whose title and theme were both inspired by the sad and sentimental saga of Abelard and Heloise.

## Nicknames of Medieval Rulers

Nicknames are found in every age of recorded history, though origins or rationale can prove difficult to uncover. During the Middle Ages nicknames often found their way into the primary source records prepared by faceless clerks and were likely unknown to the person they named.

Tradition has it that the next to the last Saxon king of England before William's successful conquest was Edward "the Confessor." The explanation that is generally accepted for this nickname is that Edward, a deeply and nervously religious man, gained needed comfort from his penitential confessions. In fact, he apparently gained so much comfort from this that when he had no transgressions to confess he simply fabricated them, which also gave him the opportunity to confess to lying. William "the Bastard," the duke of Normandy who is better known as William "the Conqueror," was illegitimate, and therefore was referred to as William the Bastard by most chroniclers and historians of the medieval period.

Nicknames often referred to a ruler's physical characteristics or even his accomplishments. William the Conqueror's father was called Robert "the Devil," and one of his early Norman ancestors was Rollo "the Red." Some of the French Carolingian kings had nicknames like "the Stammerer," "the Fat," and "the Bald." The Danes provide us with Harold "Harefoot," Erik "Bloodaxe," and Harald "Bluetooth"; the French with Philip "the Handsome" and John "the Fearless"; the Germans with Frederick "Barbarossa," which means Redbeard; and the English with John "Lackland" (all of the royal lands had been appointed to his three brothers before he was born) and Edward I "Longshanks." Many historians believe the famous Mongol conqueror of the late fourteenth century is conveniently called Tamerlane as a Western translation of "Timur the Lame," a name deriving from his deformed leg.

# Tragic Persecution of Jews in Medieval England

During the second half of the eleventh century a small but prosperous Jewish minority had developed in England due to migration that had been encouraged by many English monarchs. By the mid-twelfth century and the time of the general preaching of the Second Crusade (1144), there appeared pockets of antagonism that sometimes led to Jews being charged with ritual murder or being taken hostage and to open violence against Jews. On the day of Richard I's (the Lion-Hearted) coronation in 1189, a London mob, inflamed with the spirit of yet a third crusade, staged an anti-Jewish riot. Benedict of York (ironically he had a Christian name), a wealthy moneylender who had come to witness the coronation, was seized and tortured into undergoing a Christian baptism.

The *Annals* of Roger of Hoveden, one of the primary sources for the period, carries the story of the culmination of this tragic trend in 1190, which led to the eradication of the entire Jewish community of York. The town's Jews had holed up in the local tower, refusing to submit to extortion as a means of gaining temporary freedom; the embattled defenders eventually decided it was better "that we should kill one another, than fall into the hands of enemies of our laws." All agreed, and each family patriarch "cut the throats of his wife and sons and daughters, and then of all his servants, and lastly his own." Jewish homes were plundered and all acknowledgments of debts due the Jews were burned.

While developments of this sort were sporadic rather than widespread, Jewish moneylenders were often the victims of outright confiscation, especially if the debtor was the king. In 1198 Pope Innocent III commanded all Christian princes to force a full remission of interest owed to Jews in preparation for the Fourth Crusade. Often Jews were forced to pay a fourth of their income in taxes while Christians paid only a tenth, and the *Cambridge Medieval History* tells us that King John extorted 66,000 marks from Jews in 1210. During the reign of Edward I (1271–1307), a man known to history as the "English Justinian," many Jews were arrested, their property was confiscated, and those who would not undergo Christian baptism were hanged.

In the uneasy intervals between such episodes, Jewish leaders and bankers prospered and many became rich. However, out of necessity, they were careful to accumulate only assets that could be easily transported if hard times came, and most tried to make sure that their wealth was inconspicuous.

## Students Use Their Knowledge of Latin

Medieval students probably employed their knowledge of Latin to unlock the delights of classical poetry or study the writings of Church fathers, but many also used the tongue for their own creative enjoyment, as evidenced by the Goliardic poets so aptly described by Helen Waddell in her *Wandering Scholars*. Though most of the poems are anonymous, the poets were named because a handsome portion of their work was dedicated to a fictitious Bishop Golias. The bawdy poems usually dwelled on wine, women, and song in a fashion that often included satirical treatment of the Holy Church's most sacred rituals. The works carry such titles as "Mass for Drinkers" and "Prayer Book for Roisterers." The following two translations of the same stanza of "Confession of Golias" offer examples of content and also show the liberties taken by each translator:

> In the public house to die
> Is my resolution;
> Let wine to my lips be nigh
> At life's dissolution:
> That will make the angels cry
> With glad elocution,
> "Grant this toper, God on high
> Grace and absolution!"

And the second translation:

> My intention is to die
> In the tavern drinking
> Wine must be at hand, for I
> Want it when I'm sinking
> Angels when they come shall cry,
> At my frailties winking:
> "Spare this drunkard, God, he's high
> Absolutely stinking!"

# Was Saint Thomas Aquinas Fat?

Both recorded history and legend contain evidence that the great seminal theologian/philosopher of the High Middle Ages, Saint Thomas Aquinas (d. 1274), was extremely obese. Tradition holds that a semicircle had to be cut into his table in order for him to manage his meals with any degree of agility. Yet, while a fresco near the church of San Marco (Venice) would suggest the truth of the legend, two full-length renditions of the saint by Fra Angelico da Fiesole (Pitti, Florence and Nicholas V Chapel at the Vatican) show a tall, strong, and well-proportioned figure.

## The Heir Is Titled Prince of Wales

During the mid-thirteenth century Wales experienced a modest ethnic revival, and in 1276 Prince Llewelyn and his brother David proclaimed autonomy, declaring war against the English. England's King Edward I (1272–1307) marched his forces into Wales, killed Llewelyn in battle, executed David, observed the effectiveness of the Welsh longbow, and negotiated the terms for future pacification. Among Welsh grievances was the demand for their own prince, one who spoke no English. Thus, at Carnarvon Castle in 1284, Edward fulfilled a promise to that effect when he presented the Welsh with his infant son who was only a few weeks old, assuring them that the child certainly spoke no English. Since that time the male heir to the English throne has usually had the title of prince of Wales. The title must be conferred by letters patent and the prince must be formally invested at Carnarvon Castle.

## Cesspit Raker: A Hazardous Occupation

An early fourteenth-century entry in the Rolls of Coroners for the city of London indicates that the death of one Richard the Raker resulted from drowning. In those days few of the common flock were known by a last name. Instead, people were more likely known by a first name followed by an identifying vocation or physical characteristic. Hence we have Wat the Tyler, and Jack Straw during the Peasant's Revolt in 1381. Richard was a "raker," but what he raked provides the interesting and repulsive aspect.

The common medieval means for disposal of human excrement and similar waste was the cesspit. Effective functioning of the cesspit was premised upon seepage, and because proper seepage depended upon the fluidity of the material, dry weather might impair the intended work of the cesspit. As a result, during dry periods someone had to rake off the crust that formed over the cesspit and also remove any larger clods that might inhibit seepage.

This was the job done by Richard. Unfortunately the large diameter of the pit required that Richard work from a long plank laid over the pit, and this particular plank proved to be rotten and gave way. Richard was discovered the following day by a fellow raker. What name might have been given to a labor union for such workers?

# Joan of Arc

The struggle between England and France known to history as the Hundred Years' War (1337–1453) afforded the French but one leader whose conduct and accomplishment they might justifiably celebrate—that of a peasant girl from a small town on the Meuse River called Domrémy. Very little of her two-year career as a leader of French troops is simply tradition; it is remarkable and interesting history, the kind that nineteenth-century French historian Jules Michelet enjoyed writing.

Her military pilgrimage, which she undertook according to the instructions of the archangel Michael (and we assume of God as well) took her from her village to the residence of the king (Charles VII) at Chinon, to Orleans where she rallied the troops and lifted the English siege of that city, to Reims where kings were sometimes anointed in the tradition established by Clovis in 481, to the defense of Compiègne where she was captured, and finally to Rouen where she stood trial for a period of several months.

Here are some of the details of her trial:

1. As a result of previous experience, the juridical wing of the Universal Church had determined that humans who claimed to have had direct communion with God or his angels were guilty of heresy, which was a crime against God, not the Church. To claim to hear voices that took precedence over God's vicar on earth was the worst of blasphemous crimes.

2. Joan of Arc's judges, a group of learned theologians and scholars headed by an inquisitor and the bishop of Beauvais, heard the trial in English-held territories that were surrounded by troops loyal to the English crown.

3. After months of interrogation, Joan of Arc broke down and, at the urging of the assigned confessor, Isambart (who had come to admire her and deemed her genuine), agreed to sign a retraction. This act brought her only grief and emotional pain, for she knew

that she had heard the voices and that her most serious crime was now a false confession. Thus she withdrew the retraction, making her something worse in the eyes of the judges—a relapsed heretic.

4.  During the trial, considerable mention was made of the fact that to fulfill her role she wore the standard clothing of the cavalry soldier, cut her hair short as a man, and did not ride sidesaddle as women did.

5.  Little notice was given to the fact that she had temporarily halted the practice of permitting a train of prostitutes to follow the army as it moved and camped or that she had successfully reduced the amount of obscenities hurled about by the soldiers.

6.  She faced her sentence, to be burned at the stake, standing against the wall of the butcher market in Rouen, with a crucifix in each hand. According to tradition an English witness observed, "We are lost, we have burned a saint."

7.  According to medieval beliefs, sorceresses and witches don't leave relics, but are completely consumed by the fire. A concrete relief on the wall of the butcher market building in Rouen is all that remains today.

By decision of an ecclesiastical court of review 25 years after her death (Pope Calixtus III, 1456), the verdict was declared unjust and void. In 1920 the Maid of Orleans came to be numbered among the saints of the Church.

# CHAPTER III

# Renaissance and Reformation Era

The historical period from the mid-fourteenth century on into the late sixteenth century witnessed a waning of many of the standards, practices, and institutions correctly termed "medieval." The developments that are associated with that time period actively contributed to the decline of the medieval world and at the same time stimulated processes that helped forge the growth of the early modern era. Increasing commerce and the expansion of cities continued apace, radically changing the entire European political scene and profoundly influencing the operational and financial practices of the Universal Church, to say nothing of the lifestyle of clergy and political rulers. Europe was stunned by a series of plagues, and gunpowder became an effective political weapon in European hands. The introduction of moveable type (Gutenberg Bible) and a new type of paper enhanced the exchange and dissemination of ideas. Many states took on a more unified or national character, and a constant growth in secular attitudes worked hand in hand with the newborn institutions of capitalism. Literate members of this era took to the study of classical Greek and Roman knowledge, which had been considered pagan; this in turn altered the medieval emphasis on the afterlife to an emphasis on the present.

A traveler in western Europe could, by 1550, easily identify the great changes brought with the Renaissance simply by observing the world around him. Owing partly to gunpowder and cannons, castles had given way to the gracious and elegantly indefensible chateaux, while construction of secular buildings outdistanced that of Gothic cathedrals. Rome was just reviving by 1500. Florence had for the previous century served as a gleaming light of commerce, banking, and cultural creativity. While nations developed commercial empires in America and Asia, Europe witnessed the shattering of medieval religious unity, a revolution that led to the politicizing of both domestic and international religious wars. Peaceful coexistence was not restored until the Peace of Westphalia in 1648. Despite the flood of gold and silver into the European economy, the expansion of commerce and available goods, and the increasing sophistication of law and government politics, the average person was much worse off in 1600 than in 1400. And no era in European history has exhibited a degree of religious hatred and intolerance to equal that of the Reformation.

## Questions for Discussion

- What did John Hus, a clergyman from Prague, do to warrant condemnation by the ecumenical Council of Constance and execution by fire?

- Give some examples of religious brutality and hatred. Were Catholics and Protestants equally guilty of hostility and prejudice?

- Why was Philip II of Spain referred to as His Most Catholic Majesty? Would you characterize him as having a sympathetic and compromising personality? Why?

- What was Philip II of Spain's reaction to the Saint Bartholomew's Day Massacre? How did the pope react to the massacre? Could it be said that during the sixteenth century just about any action was justifiable as long as it was done in the name of the "true faith"?

- Florence was the shining jewel of cultural vitality, artistic creativity, and economic prosperity during the fifteenth century. What did the careers of Lorenzo de Medici, the Dominican Savonarola, and the popes illustrate in terms of the quality of life in Italy?

- Was syphilis a product of the New or the Old World? How serious was the disease's impact in the sixteenth century?

- How did Sir Thomas More demonstrate his faith and rectitude as a Christian at his own execution?

- What problems did Henry VIII of England have with the women in his life? Why was a divorce from Catherine of Aragon so important to Henry as king of England?

- In what ways did the famous court of the Star Chamber differ from standard common law courts, and what types of cases made its functions unique?

- What factors of human conduct made a crop like tobacco so valuable even though it could not be used for food? What factors should be considered when looking at the increased consumption of gin and rum in the centuries following the Age of Exploration?

- How is the Universal Church indebted to the career of Ignatius Loyola?

# The Relics of Europe

Relics were intended to serve as instruments for instruction, particularly to engender Christian virtue, conduct, and holiness. These tools multiplied in number, use, and abuse during the Middle Ages; by the time of Luther (1500s) relics had become the subject of criticism by serious scholars. Some of the more exotic examples of such relics were the foreskin of John the Baptist and glass vials containing portions of the darkness that God cast over Egypt during the reign of Rameses II. Traffic in and collection of relics were very common, and by Luther's time there had been consigned to each holy item a measured benefit or indulgence value, most commonly a reduction in the amount of time to be spent in purgatory. Valuable possessions of various churches in Rome included the bodies of 40 popes and 76,000 martyrs, who were buried in the crypt of Saint Callistus; a piece of the burning bush seen by Moses; a true portrait of Jesus on the napkin of Saint Veronica; the scissors with which Emperor Domitian clipped Saint John's hair; the walls near the Appian gate, which showed white spots supposedly left by the stones that had turned to snowballs when a mob hurled them at Saint Peter; a crucifix that had leaned over to talk to Saint Brigitta; one of the coins paid to Judas for betraying Jesus (this relic conveyed an indulgence value of 1,400 years); the 12-foot beam from which Judas hanged himself; and the sacred stairs near Saint John Lateran, 28 in all, that once stood in front of Pontius Pilate's palace—if one crawled up on hands and knees, repeating a paternoster for each step, a soul would be released from purgatory (assuming of course the supplicant was genuinely contrite).

At the time of Luther the holy possessions of Frederick the Wise of Saxony included a thorn that had pierced Jesus' brow; a tooth of Saint Jerome; four pieces of Chrysostom, six pieces of Saint Bernard, and four pieces of Saint Augustine; four hairs from the Virgin Mary, three pieces of her cloak, four of her girdle, and seven of her veil, which were sprinkled with the blood of Jesus; one piece of Jesus' swaddling clothes, thirteen of his crib, one wisp of straw from the manger, one piece of the gold that had been brought by the Wise Men, one piece of bread served at the Last Supper, one strand of Jesus' beard, one of the nails driven into his hands, and one piece of the stone on which Jesus was standing when he ascended into heaven; and one twig of the burning bush seen by Moses. By 1520, Frederick the Wise's collection had mounted to 19,013 holy items with a combined indulgence value designated at 1,902,202 years and 270 days.

## The Black Death

The Great Plague of 1348–1349 was merely the worst of periodic European epidemics, for pestilence was a normal incident in the Middle Ages. The Great Plague carried off no less than one-fourth of the general population (killing possibly as many as 25 million), but in some locations it even wiped out whole towns. The plague was not partial to rank or wealth: According to G. G. Coulton, of 28 cardinals alive in 1348, 9 were dead a year later; of 64 archbishops, 25 died; of 375 bishops, 207 died. The young and the undernourished were especially susceptible.

In the introduction to his *Decameron* Boccaccio described the symptoms: dark blotches under the flesh, lumps in the areas of armpits, groin, or throat, and death after a few days of suffering. He also described the varied reactions of the uninfected. Some shut themselves in their homes, refusing contact with family or loved ones, yet were still struck down by the disease. Others declared that no medicine was of value and resorted to drinking and pursuit of pleasure to fill the short time they believed was left to them. Some simply fled to the forests while others remained, moving about among the dead carcasses with nosegays of flowers, herbs, and spices as a defense against the smell. As it was often the grave-diggers and coffin-bearers who died first, the horror of unburied human and animal bodies grew in quantity.

## Two Significant Renaissance Inventions

The Gutenberg Bible dates from 1456 and demonstrates the effectiveness of moveable type in the process of printing. Prior to the fifteenth century, the skins of 300 sheep were required to print a single Bible. When the new printing methods that resulted from moveable type were combined with the development of paper production (c. 1450), the result was an explosion of what historians call cultural diffusion. Within 50 years the new presses had produced a total of 6 million books, and a total of 400,000 works. It was thus easier for the Luthers of the sixteenth century to render an impact.

Gunpowder is said to have begun as a carnival toy in China. It moved from there through the Arab world to the west, where it became a political weapon that encouraged the construction of elegant chateaux (refined living) while ending the construction of castles (defense bastions). It became militarily impratical to put great effort and expense into structures whose walls and other defenses could be easily breached by cannon fire. Thus, the great structures of the fifteenth and sixteenth centuries tended to be secular and either civic or elegant in purpose or function. The great chateaux of France's Loire Valley stand as Renaissance architectural testimony to the presence of cannon. For the first time during the entire medieval period, the walls of Constantinople were breached in 1453, because of cannon. The use of gunpowder also spurred mining and improvements in metallurgy for the casting of cannons, which in turn both changed the style of warfare and increased the cost. It also rendered the whole concept of medieval-style chivalry (as exemplified in the *Song of Roland*) defunct. It was not an accident of history that in the battle of Pavia in 1525 the forces of France lost 8,000 while the imperial forces of Charles V (equipped with gunpowder) lost but 800.

## Brutality in Renaissance Italy

The Visconti family that ruled Milan and much of northern Italy by the late fourteenth century included some of the cruelest people known to history. Uncle Bernabo taxed his subjects without mercy, indulged himself in the hunt with the aid of the 5,000 hunting dogs he kept, and quieted resentment to his rule by announcing that all criminals would automatically be subjected to 40 days of torture. His nephew Giangaleazzo, known for piety, invited Bernabo and his two sons to a meeting, arrested all three, and apparently poisoned Bernabo. Giangaleazzo then expanded his rule to a dozen northern cities, but died prematurely at age 52, in 1402. His son Gianmaria left administration to rival generals, and while they engaged in intermittent war, he devoted himself to his dogs, which he trained to eat human flesh. He then took pleasure in watching them feed on live political offenders and common criminals. In 1412 three members of the aristocracy stabbed him to death.

## Council of Constance:
## The Clergy Punish a Critic

The purposes of the Council of Constance (1414–1417), a meeting of the most important clergymen and also many laymen, were to end the papal schism (two simultaneous popes), to organize the governance of the Church for the future, and to develop a plan to have similar meetings with regularity. A sidelight to the great conclave was the criticism of one John Hus, a Bohemian scholar from Prague who had for several years spoken out against the tendencies of priests who violated their vows. Hus asserted that priests who lived profligate lives were incapable of performing the roles of their office, and that sacraments delivered by such priests would have no value.

For the sake of solving the dispute caused by this issue, Emperor Sigismund had promised "safe conduct" to Hus so that he might present his views at the important meeting. Though the meeting had not been called to deal with Hus's accusations, the treatment he received is of historical interest. Before sessions of the Council commenced at Constance in 1414, the clergy attending (cardinals, archbishops, bishops, and others) were advised that all prostitutes were to be kept outside the city and that all clergy were required to arrive at the sessions sober. These were some of the very behaviors that John Hus had criticized. After hearing Hus speak, the Council condemned him as a heretic. He was sentenced to death and burned at the stake.

# Growing Secularism in Florentine Politics

Historians often refer to the Middle Ages as the Age of Faith and describe the Renaissance as an era of growing secularism. The examples of this increasing secularism are conspicuous. The construction of chateaux and civic structures, the expansion of trade in consumer goods, the study of pagan classics, and the growth in banking, armies, and warfare all indicate an ever-expanding secular demeanor that Sir Thomas More certainly had in mind when he wrote his *Utopia*. The following are two somewhat extreme examples of that trend, both taken from the period when Florence was at the peak of her power and cultural influence.

## The Pazzi Plot

In 1478 a plot was laid by the Pazzi family of Florence to seize control from the Medici family, who had been successful and held supreme power for some time. Accomplices included the local archbishop, the Salviati, and the pope himself, Sixtus IV. The conspirators planned to assassinate Lorenzo "the Magnificent" and his brother Guiliano, storm city hall (Palazzo Vecchio), turn out the council members, and then await the rewards of a papal victory.

The plot was a disastrous failure, but some aspects of the affair reveal much about the state of religious sanctity in Renaissance Italy. First, the attempted assassination was not only arranged for Easter Sunday services in the cathedral, but the actual attack occurred as the priest blessed the bread at the very core of Holy Communion. Second, when the conspirators assigned to city hall failed to gain entrance the mob and loyal Medici supporters entered the fray, and there ensued an ugly episode that ended with one Pazzi and an archbishop hanging from the first level of city hall while the populace stoned them. Third, though Pope Sixtus had refused to be a part of the assassination, he was aware of it, and he subsequently excommunicated the Medicis and their followers. (This is the same pope for whom was named and dedicated the Sistine Chapel.) And fourth, Florentines ignored the excommunication and carried on life as usual.

## Savonarola's Rise and Fall

During the 1490s the greatest threat to both Medici rule in Florence and papal primacy in the Church came from a Dominican monk and popular sermonizer named Girolamo Savonarola. In fiery sermons Savonarola attacked the very secular practices that so characterized much of the civilization of the Renaissance—overriding interests in makeup, jewelry, works of art, music, colorful dress, festivals, and games and the Medici wealth. His sermons were soon such attractions that standing-room crowds thronged the major cathedral and women were being turned away. His targets came to include even the papal office and the conduct of popes; he often criticized their wealth, their nepotism, their practice of keeping concubines, and their tendencies to appoint their bastard sons as cardinals. An attempt to silence him with a cardinal's hat met with refusal. Ordered by Pope Alexander VI to cease preaching, Savonarola only expanded his mission, successfully predicted the natural death of Lorenzo de Medici, and then made the fatal step, the same one that had transformed so many reformers into heretics: He claimed to be acting on the direct wishes of God.

After Lorenzo died as predicted, those under Savonarola's leadership seized control of Florence. Secular treasures, books, paintings, and clothing were burned in huge bonfires in the public square before the Palazzo Vecchio. But not all Florentines were Savonarola fans. He certainly had no supporters among extravagant clergymen, who were threatened by his puritanism. And many others tired of the austere rule of his party and longed for the gaiety and splendor of the Medici era. Ultimately the Dominican was challenged to prove that he was God's messenger and demonstrate that he enjoyed God's protection. The test was to walk through fire unscathed by its heat, which the Franciscans agreed to do as well on the condition that Savonarola would do so first. Savonarola accepted, but then slowly backed away from the roaring flames as the amassed population of Florence looked on. The mob was disappointed; as a result, the monks' quarters at San Marco were stormed, Savonarola and his two closest aides were seized, and he was forthwith tried in the fashion of the Inquisition. Each of the three was tortured until he made the appropriate confession: Savonarola was not really God's arm, they had heard no voices, and hence they were guilty of both schism and heresy.

On May 23, 1498, in the square before the towering Palazzo Vecchio, on the very spot where the monk and his followers had burned the "vanities," the three men were hanged from a gibbet and boys were allowed to stone them as they choked. Then, as was the custom for heretics, a giant fire was lighted beneath them so that they would leave no traces save ashes, all of which were thrown into the River Arno. The victory of secularism was not lost on a young man named Martin Luther when he visited Italy. He felt he had never seen a place so devoid of holiness.

# Syphilis: A Product of the New World or the Old?

Whether or not syphilis existed in Europe before Columbus returned in 1493 remains a matter of debate. Among the facts that indicate European origin are the following:

A prostitute in a court at Dijon admitted that she suffered from *le gros mal*

In 1494 Paris ordered from the city all persons afflicted with *la grosse verole*

There was an epidemic of a disease with identical symptoms in Naples after the French invasion of that city in 1494, causing Italians to refer to the disease as *il morbo gallico* (the French disease)

French soldiers returning from Italy spread the disease to various areas of France, where it became known as *le mal de Naples*

Even before French soldiers began to return from the campaign in Italy, the Holy Roman Emperor of Germany issued an edict regarding the *malum francicum*

From 1500 onward the disease was commonly described throughout Europe as *morbus gallicus*

The belief that syphilis originated in the New World, as described by Castiglione in his *History of Medicine,* is largely due to an attack of the disease suffered by a pilot aboard one of Columbus's return vessels and also by a number of other sailors, in Barcelona, who were soon after treated for the disease. As well, few archaeological studies of pre-Columbian bones from Europe have revealed the presence of the syphilis strain, while many such bones of pre-Columbian America suggest the presence of the disease there.

In any case, syphilis spread rapidly in the sixteenth century and we have ample evidence that many cardinals, Caesar Borgia, and even Pope Julius II (1503–1513) were infected. It was indeed the epidemic of the century, reaching all the way to King Henry VIII of England and, as some have claimed, even causing infertility in both Mary Tudor and Queen Elizabeth I.

The name *syphilis* originated with an Italian professor, scientist, and medical researcher who was fond of classical literature. He wrote a poem modeled on classical themes in which Apollo afflicts a shepherd, who had chosen to worship other gods, with a disease. The story is similar to the affliction of Job; the author of the poem (Girolamo Fracastoro) describes the disease's symptoms as ulcerated skin, pustules, infection of the bones, and occasionally complete consumption of the sex organs. The shepherd of the story is from the ancient region of Syphilus. To treat the disease, which even Fracastoro called *morbo gallico,* either mercury or extract from guaiacum—a "holy wood" used by American Indians—was prescribed.

# Leonardo da Vinci's Sexual Preference

A good deal of scholarship and commentary has been devoted to establishing whether or not Leonardo da Vinci was a homosexual. There is no reason to believe that conclusive evidence will ever be found about one whose creative career began in 1474 and only ended with his death in 1519, while he was in the service of the French royal family. (Authorities at

Amboise, France, claim he is buried behind the altar of the chapel near the chateau entrance.)

Historian Rachel Taylor confirms reports that da Vinci was twice charged with having homosexual relations with other youths during his mid-20s, but there is neither a record of the charge being proved nor of any sentence being given. Many historians believe da Vinci probably was homosexual, for as soon as he could afford to he established a studio, staffed it entirely with handsome young men, traveled only in the company of men, and referred to some of them in his correspondence as "most beloved" or "dearest." But there are other historians who, based upon some of da Vinci's writings, believe the artist found sexuality and sexual acts of any kind to be generally repulsive; thus these historians consider him asexual. Da Vinci occasionally referred to the body's "violent parts" and said that "members employed" in the act of procreation are "so repulsive." A definite answer to this puzzle is yet to be found.

## *Sodoma: A Prominent Artist Earns a Name*

One of the brightest and most revered artistic talents of Renaissance Siena was Giovanni Antonio Bazzi (1477–1549), who worked there most of his adult life except for a period of service with two popes in Rome. While his works can be found among the works of masters such as Raphael, his pieces are identified not by his given name but by his cognomen, Sodoma. He earned the nickname by his open and scandalous sexual behavior. He accepted the name in good humor, and spent much of his time living up to it. His conduct became too much even for the "Warrior Pope," Julius II, who employed him and later, in disgust, released him from service. He later worked for Pope Leo X (1513–1521), painting for him a nude Lucretia stabbing herself, for which Leo paid him well and made him a Cavalier of the Order of Christ. An Italian historian who lived during this period, Giorgio Vasari, said of Bazzi: "His manner of life was licentious and dishonorable; and as he always had boys and beardless youth about him, of whom he was inordinately fond, this earned him the name of Sodoma. Instead of feeling shame, he gloried in it, writing verses about it, and singing them to the accompaniment of the lute."

## The Personality of Martin Luther

The German reformer (d. 1546), who nailed his famous 95 Theses to a church door in Wittenberg and so gave the opening signal to one of the greatest religious revolutions in all history, exhibited many attributes of his era. He was certainly out of step with most of the popular practices and theological policies of the Church, but in many ways he was a rather typical German of simple roots.

He believed in demons and evil spirits, just as his mother did. He even threw his inkwell at such evil intruders as they approached him late one night while he worked by candlelight. Once, while in the choir loft with other Augustinian clergy, he was personally gripped by an evil spirit with which he wrestled feverishly and eventually cast off.

Once the final break with the Roman Catholic Church had been made, he offered no compromise on any issue and resorted to the most basic of peasant verbiage to state his case. When Henry VIII defended the Church's seven sacraments against Luther's writings, the reformer responded by calling the king a pig, and said, "I will bespatter him with his own dung."

Luther claimed that man should rule woman, but with kindness. He looked upon women as creatures with a specific place—essentially to remain in the home and behave as servants—and suggested that women would be wise to recite the Lord's Prayer before opening their mouths. Should God take women during childbirth, that too was part of God's plan; after all, "that [giving birth] is what they are for."

## The Death of Thomas More

For obvious political reasons, Henry VIII could not permit Sir Thomas More to evade accepting the king in his new role as "head" of the English Church. There was no more respected man in the realm than the king's former chancellor and eminent jurist; and the stability of Henry's realm, the succession to the crown, and the legality of his divorce and new marriage were threatened by More's refusal to swear an oath of loyalty to the king in "all his titles." An example had to be set. Thus, in his final trial the humanist-scholar was pronounced guilty of treason, a crime for which the sentence was virtually automatic. More used the day before his execution to bid good-bye to his wife and daughter and all his friends. On the morning of his execution, he declared that it was a fine day to meet God. When he climbed the scaffold it shook as though ready to collapse, and he told the attendant, "I pray you, Mr. Lieutenant, see me safe up, and for my coming down let me shift for myself." Historian J. A. Froude tells us that among his last statements More asserted that he died the king's good servant, but God's first. As he laid his head upon the cutting block he carefully arranged his long gray beard, saying, "Pity that should be cut, that hath not committed treason." His head was placed atop a spike on London Bridge in accordance with the legal practice of *terrorum populi.*

## Sixteenth-Century Religious Hatred

The animosities brought on by the spread of Protestant ideas spread quickly to other countries in the years that followed the posting of Luther's 95 Theses in 1517. In 1523 a wool-carder from the city of Meaux tore down a papal bull of indulgences that had been posted by the bishop, then replaced it with a placard that called the pope an Antichrist. The wool-carder, Jean Leclerc, was arrested and branded on the forehead. He then moved to Metz, where he went on a rampage and smashed religious images before a city ceremonial procession. For this his hand was cut off, his nose was torn away, his nipples were plucked off with pincers, and his head was bound with a band of red-hot iron. Leclerc was finally burned alive in 1526.

On the eve of Saint Bartholomew's Day, August 24, 1572, the aristocratic cream of France gathered in Paris for the wedding that would join the royal houses of Bourbon (Protestant) and Valois (Catholic and the ruling dynasty). At 3:00 A.M. the following morning, by a prearranged plot, the Catholic adherents rose up and launched a full day of slaughter of the Protestants, which took 5,000 lives. When the news reached Philip II of Spain, who was known as His Most Catholic Majesty, the austere monarch reportedly laughed out loud, unusual behavior for him. The papal nuncio said, "Blessed be God," and offered congratulations for such a noble action. In Rome the news was greeted by the continuous ringing of bells, and Pope Pius I (1566–1572) had a special medal struck to commemorate the blessed occasion.

In another example of religious intolerance, John Knox (1505–1572), the founder and propagator of Protestantism in Scotland, attacked women Catholic rulers in a pamphlet entitled "First Blast of the Trumpet Against the Monstrous Regiment of Women." In this pamphlet he called Mary Tudor a whore and a Jezebel. Knox asserted that the thirteenth chapter of Deuteronomy should be obeyed, suggesting that true believers (puritanical Protestants like himself) were obligated by God's command to put to death all heretics and to destroy to the last house and animal any and all cities that were predominantly heretical. Of course, he heaped heavy abuse on his own ruler, the pathetic and unfortunate Mary, Queen of Scots, and at one point said to her, "Madame, thou art dung before the Lord."

One anti-Catholic myth that received great attention in Protestant popular literature centered upon the existence of the Popess Joanna. Wrote one outspoken Protestant, "People could see and know what double-dyked knaves and villains the Jesuiwiders [Jesuits] were, for they attempted to deny that the English whore Agnes had been popess at Rome and had given birth to a boy during a public procession." Others in their sermons consistently levied propagandist attacks on popes, charging that they were sodomites, necromancers, and magicians who often communed directly with Satan and performed naked dances over the cross of Jesus.

# Erasmus: Critic of His Society

While contemporary scholars would have readily conceded to Desiderius Erasmus (1466?–1536) the title of dean of the northern humanists, most modern scholars of cultural history regularly make reference to an Age of Erasmus. He was unique in both his consistent honesty and his absolute refusal to play the hypocrite. His writings spanned a broad spectrum of current affairs, philosophy, religion, classical scholarship, and witty polemics. No pen produced sharper barbs for the wicked of his lifetime, be they king or pope. Paramount among his targets were monks who repeatedly violated their vows, Christian rulers who waged war against other Christians, popes who devoted more effort to war and gold than to the needs of their flock, and the educated who, because of their learning, should have known that God did not reserve wisdom and tolerance to Christians alone.

Some of his writings were dangerously specific:

1. In the satirical *Julius Exclusus*, we find Pope Julius II (1503–1513), known to history as the Warrior Pope, in a dialogue with Saint Peter before heaven's gate. The pope's key does not fit the gate because he has mistakenly brought the one he used most—the key to his money chest. He is insulted when Saint Peter takes the large P.M. on his vestments to mean *Pestis Maxima* instead of *Pontifex Maximus*, after which the gate's guardian claims that it is indeed difficult to recognize as a pope someone who smells of brothels, booze, and gunpowder and has just puked from his own excesses. Though the work was written anonymously a year after Julius died, the manuscript circulated widely and all the learned recognized the hand.

2. Erasmus used his *Praise of Folly* to argue that so much of what makes humankind tick is devoid of reason, wisdom, calculation, or intellect. On the contrary, he saw everywhere in human conduct the heavy stamp of folly, ignorance, and stupidity, along with impulse, instinct, and emotion. He asserted that if it were not for man's unreasoned and feverish lust after woman's flesh, his "goatish passion for copulation," the human race would be lost. What would happen if at the point when a woman's mind turned to sex she immediately was gripped by the pains and tribulations of birth and motherhood? He also lampooned monks, friars, inquisitors, cardinals, and popes, and concluded that popes had become so busy with riches, palaces, honors, offices, indulgences, and other powers that they did not even slightly resemble the Apostles, saying that bloody wars are what popes know best.

3. His *Colloquies*, which examined a wide range of subjects and shocked equally both Martin Luther and Emperor Charles V, carried on the attack. He condemned relic-mongering, misuse of excommunication, false miracles used to deceive the unlettered, the cult of saints, and the conspicuous differences between the Christianity of Jesus and the contemporary international monster presided over by a lavish and opulent clergy. He had prostitutes praise monks as their best clients, charged that chastity was more endangered inside than outside the cloister, referred to monks as "swill-bellied" and in search of riches, and offered a special

blessing to be used upon meeting a pregnant woman—"Heaven grant that this burden you carry . . . may have as easy an exit as it had an entrance."

Also in his *Colloquies,* Erasmus described how he joined the English humanist John Colet on a pilgrimage to the shrine of Saint Thomas Becket at Canterbury. Though employing fictitious names, Erasmus related how offended their monastic guide had been by Colet's suggestion that some of the wealth that adorned the cathedral might be used to mitigate the suffering of the poor who wandered the surrounding streets. He went on to report the large quantity of bones that required kissing, the observation of some milk that had come from the Virgin's breast, and how Colet had shuddered and refused to kiss a shoe that the saint had worn. Finally, when the monastic guide offered a souvenir cloth that held Becket's sweat and nostril mucus, Colet asserted that the time was short and they had to leave for London.

# Gargantua: Rabelais Describes a Renaissance Man

Today a large appetite might be described by a single word: gargantuan. The term derives from the central character in the mid-fifteenth-century writings of François Rabelais. By profession a physician, and well traveled owing to service with important dignitaries (for example, Jean du Bellay, the bishop of Paris), Rabelais wrote stories about the genial giant Gargantua and his son Pantagruel that offered the same rollicking satire of the clergy that is contained in Boccaccio's *Decameron.* Only the Bible and the *Lamentations of Christ* outsold his stories among contemporary publications; they earned the condemnation of clerical scholars at the Sorbonne and the laughter and applause of King Francis I (1515–1547).

Gargantua, who had been carried in the womb of his mother, Garganuelle, for eleven months, had a thirst for life: As he climbed through his mother's diaphragm and neck and out by way of "the left ear," his first three words were "Drink! Drink! Drink!" The words were delivered so loudly that two countries heard them. Rabelais gave this giant what many might call the spirit of the

Renaissance, stressing a revival in learning and an emphasis on the rewards of this life. We find Gargantua on one occasion in a stream at its widest point. He is on his back, propelling himself about the water's surface by kicking his feet. In one hand he holds the apple he is eating and in the other he holds an open Latin primer. In this episode we have physical exercise, nourishment of the body, and nourishment of the mind. The message was not new, it was merely delivered on a more popular level than was the case with Pico and his *Oration on the Dignity of Man.*

## *The Tragic Fate of Four Explorers*

Most students are familiar with the name Henry Hudson, who, after attempts at discovering a northeast polar passage to China for the Muscovey Company, sailed for the Dutch West India Company to seek a northwest passage. His efforts in the latter case formed the basis for the Dutch claim to New York (New Amsterdam was later lost to the British). His work for the British established that nation's claim to Hudson's Bay, but he had still not found a passage to China. What students seldom learn is that on his last voyage, after another failure and with winter setting in, his crew mutinied. Hudson, his young son, the sick, and the faithful members of his crew were set adrift in a small open boat and never seen again. The remainder of the sailors took the ship back to England, where they escaped punishment.

Another explorer, Vasco Nuñez de Balboa, was a stowaway fleeing creditors in Santo Domingo when he successfully usurped royal authority, seized power in the region of Panama, sent home the royally appointed governor, established a new and successful colony at Darien, and discovered the Pacific Ocean. Balboa was planning a voyage across that body of water when he was arrested and executed by a brutal royal agent named Pedrarias.

It was actually the remaining members of Ferdinand Magellan's crew, and not the explorer himself, who successfully circum-navigated the world between 1519 and 1522. Magellan sailed in September of 1519 with five ships, reached South America, lost one ship, quelled a mutiny, navigated the strait that bears his name, and then spent more than four months in the Pacific. By the time they reached the Philippine Islands the crew had been

ى a diet of leather and ship rats. It was there that
لan became involved in a quarrel between two native chief-
لıs and was killed. When his successor, Juan Sebastian de
Elcano, finally completed the voyage, arriving with but one ship
left, it had taken three years. But the value of the cargo still
produced a profit for the entire undertaking.

Francisco Pizarro, whom one historian has called an ethical and
moral Neanderthal, was a 61-year-old illiterate son of a peasant
when he led about 600 Spaniards in an attack against the Inca
Empire in 1541. Aided by an internal struggle among the Incas for
their crown, Pizarro was able to capture the new victorious Inca
ruler. Ransom for the Inca's freedom was a room filled with
golden dishes, and, when the sum had been collected, Pizarro
treacherously strangled the Inca leader. Soon afterward a
fratricidal struggle among the Spanish party erupted and in the
resulting quarrel Pizarro was murdered.

## *Henry VIII and Women*

It is probably safe to say that no divorce (or annulment) in history
has received as much attention as the dissolution of the marriage
between Henry VIII (1509–1547) and his Spanish queen Catherine
of Aragon, which was effected to make room for Anne Boleyn and
a hoped-for male heir to the English throne. Historians agree that
the essential motivation was political, which was obviously
understood by the majority of Henry's Parliaments. There were
some interesting and ironic developments because of the
annulment, aside from the fact that Henry ultimately went on to
marry no less than five more times:

1.  The offspring of the first marriage, Mary Tudor (who would later
    become queen), was declared illegitimate, which meant that
    Catherine was a prostitute and Mary a bastard. Mary was placed
    in a home under the supervision of Anne Boleyn's aunt, who was
    instructed to keep "the bastard in place with a box on the ear."

2.  Henry was certainly infatuated with Anne Boleyn, but for reasons
    unknown to historians. She had a plain face, an inordinately long
    neck, a gangly body, a sixth finger on one hand, and a large cherry

birthmark on her throat. Her pregnancy obviously aided her rise to the throne, but she never produced the male child (only Elizabeth, who would become queen) so feverishly sought. She later became irritable, bitchy (criticizing the king's eating habits in front of foreign ambassadors), and given to tantrums, all of which produced no results. She was subsequently convicted of adultery (this was treason if willfully done by royalty) and executed in the Tower of London. Parliament then drafted legislation to render Anne's daughter, Elizabeth, a bastard.

3. Jane Seymour, Henry's third wife, finally produced the desired male heir but died during childbirth. That child became Edward VI, who as a youth had such ill health that Parliament was forced to legitimize both Mary and Elizabeth in case of his death, an event that came after five years' rule, at age 15.

4. Henry's fourth wife, Anne of Cleves, was chosen after Henry received an inaccurately flattering portrait of her by Hans Holbein, and diplomatic arrangements were made by Chancellor Thomas Cromwell. When Henry met her at the wharf he was so shocked and displeased that it was all his aides could do to keep him there and get him to perform his duties. Henry never forgave Holbein, and Cromwell was later executed for treason.

5. After he had divorced Anne of Cleves, whom Henry referred to in front of his cronies as his "Flemish mare," wife number five, Catherine Howard, was executed for adultery. The king's sixth wife, Catherine Parr, outlived him.

## Interesting Cases in the Star Chamber

Contrary to legend, the English court of the Star Chamber was not secretive, brutal, or sinister, nor did it employ harsh and irregular procedures. It was in fact a hard-working court with personnel similar to that of other courts, but it was the court that applied equity rulings. It dealt with cases requiring redress or remedy in situations that were not yet part of statute laws and that had no judicial precedent in common law. Much of its work entailed what we would today call fraud—diluting wine, use of false weights and measures, concocted monopoly of goods, and slander. The Star Chamber also heard most of the more unusual cases, and the following examples are selected from English *State Trials* to demonstrate that point.

During the reign of Henry VIII a chap named Sherfield was convicted of a crime and ordered to pay a large fine of 500 pounds (about $25,000). Sherfield had deliberately and openly smashed a large stained glass window in Saint Edmund's Church in Salisbury. As the testimony reveals, the window had contained a representation of the creation of Eve; Sherfield, a serious student of and believer in the Scripture, felt that the portrayal was improper (inaccurate). To him the window was a visual blasphemy, a violation of God's law, and hence had to be destroyed.

In the fifth year of the reign of Elizabeth I, 1563, the records show that the Earl of Hartford was fined the enormous sum of 5,000 pounds ($250,000) "for deflowering Lady Catherine Grey." However, this was not a case involving a charge of rape, for then the common law courts would have heard it, as they had since Anglo-Saxon times. It appears that family redress was sought for an occurrence that might have been postponed to a later date had the good earl been less hasty or aggressive. As with other punishments, the purpose of large fines in such cases was to discourage observers from engaging in such activities. In reality, most fines were of a more manageable amount.

In the thirteenth year of the reign of Henry VI, 1412, one William Blakely was sentenced to pillory and forced to wear a heavy whetstone hung around his neck. William had been found guilty of pretending to be a hermit. The court, (we assume with aid of witnesses and affidavits) knew the accused to be by occupation a shuttlemaker. However, he had recently begun to wander through the streets with bare feet and had permitted his hair to grow long in the guise of pictured saints; he had represented himself to strangers as a pilgrim who had visited Jerusalem, Rome, Venice, and Seville, and as a result had "received many good things from divers people." All the court did was halt William from playing upon the religious susceptibilities of the innocent or uninformed. If William's actions had already been known to common law, a simple writ to "cease and desist" would have done the job. In this way the Star Chamber provided for a living and growing law.

# Did Queen Mary Deserve To Be Called "Bloody"?

The name by which history so often refers to Mary Tudor (1553–1558) is largely the result of Protestant propaganda fomented during the sixteenth and seventeenth centuries, a good deal of it spread by the popular *Book of Martyrs*, which was compiled by John Fox during his exile from England. In truth, approximately 300 people lost their lives as a result of religious persecution under Mary, a rather small number when contrasted to the situation on the Continent, where religious struggles often led to the elimination of whole towns. However, the English victims did include several high-profile Protestants. There were three bishops: Hooper, Ridley, and Latimer. Thomas Cranmer, the archbishop who approved the divorce that temporarily made Mary a bastard, has received the greatest attention. The *Book of Martyrs* leads us to believe that he signed a recantation of his Protestant views under severe torture, professing belief in all the sacraments and all essential teachings of the Roman Catholic Church. Then, when he was burned at the stake, he placed his hand directly into the flames so the limb that signed the recantation might be consumed first.

Historians often feel sympathetic toward Mary. She faced many adversities early in life, and there was also a challenge-conspiracy against her ascension to the throne. The only man she ever loved was Philip II of Spain, who disliked her and only married her for political reasons. Although he promised to return to her after his wars in the Netherlands were over, he reneged on the promise. Even her pregnancy turned out to be false.

# An Ambassador's Legacy

In 1550 the French ambassador to Portugal presented some seeds to his queen, Catherine de Medici, so that her royal gardener in Paris might grow for her some of the plants discovered and cultivated in the New World colonies of Portugal. His name was Jean Nicot; the organic compound found throughout the plant, but especially in the leaves, is called nicotine. Even the proper botanical term for the plant bears his name: *Nicotina tabacum.*

## Philip II of Spain, Most Catholic of Majesties

The son of Holy Roman Emperor and king of Spain Charles V, Philip II (1555–1598) inherited a kingdom, a New World empire, and a commission to eradicate the Protestant infection that threatened to destroy the very body of Europe and the one sure truth of the Universal Church. His maternal grandmother was Juana la Loca, the insane daughter of Ferdinand the Catholic. He was reared and educated by priests and women and grew to a man of great inner strength, most of which was channeled into a fanatical bigotry and an austere mystical rectitude. He believed that only Catholicism could save Europe and that there must be no compromise with heretics.

It was for such reasons that he married Mary Tudor of England, 11 years his senior, and attempted to make her pregnant. He wanted to surround the Protestant enemies harbored in France and the Netherlands and preserve England as a Catholic state. Even Philip's royal palace complex near Madrid reflected the stern religious devotion that moved him. What we know today as Escorial was purposely designed to atone for his sins of previous battles.

The palace is laid out like a gridiron, with crisscrossing halls that represent the iron grid on which Saint Lawrence was burned by his persecutors. In Philip's day the halls were sombre, and one would have noticed the regular movement of clergy in hooded robes, their faces hidden in mystical silence as they carried out their duties. And need we mention the wealth and work that went into the great Armada, and its intended purpose?

## Catherine de Medici, Manipulating Queen Mother

Catherine de Medici was born in Florence, in 1519, to parents who both died of syphilis before she was a month old. Joined to Henry

II (1547–1559) of France in a political marriage at age 14, she subsequently bore ten children, three of whom became kings and two who became queens. Her reign as queen and then as queen mother spanned the most brutal and fratricidal period of the French religious struggles between Protestant and Catholic armies, a struggle inflamed by outside aid to both factions.

Henry II died in 1559, in a jousting tournament, when his eye and brain were pierced with the splinter from a broken lance. All three of Catherine's sons were sickly and weak, and she manipulated royal policies and persons as if she had read Machiavelli before she was born. The first son to rule, who was also the first husband of Mary, Queen of Scots, died within a year. The second, Charles IX (1560–1574), the sickliest of the three, had a penchant for cruelty and a temper that occasionally bordered upon insanity. Between these extremes of behavior he had no mind of his own and was putty in Catherine's hands. It was he who presided over the Saint Bartholomew's Day Massacre (1572), after being cajoled and pressured for hours by Catherine and the ultra-Catholic Guise faction.

The third son to rule, Henry III (1574–1588), by his very personal proclivities, guaranteed that the struggle to control the direction of the crown would be heightened, because it was clear that there would be an empty throne to fill. He was physically weak, emotionally unstable, tired easily, and avoided physical activities. He suffered from incurably itchy skin, chronic headaches and stomachaches, and an ear that drained incessantly. By the age of 36 his hair was white and his teeth were gone. He had a passion for women's clothing and appeared at celebrations and balls in low-necked dresses, wearing pearls around his neck and sporting earrings and bracelets. Several young dandies gave him constant company, all of whom frizzed their long hair, wore makeup, adorned themselves with elegant feminine clothing, and employed good amounts of perfume. He insisted on the comfort of a lapdog to pet, and for entertainment often played garden games with his dandies, in which they all pretended to be different flowers. Obviously, there was to be no heir from this quarter, and this fact stimulated the drive of both Protestant and Catholic factions.

In the final convulsive years of the struggle, Henry III had the leader of the ultra-Catholic Guise faction murdered and designated the Protestant leader, Henry Bourbon, as his heir. Then, a short time later, a religious fanatic treacherously entered the royal camp and stabbed Henry III in the stomach. And in the name of the true faiths, France continued to bleed.

## Loyola and the Jesuit Order

Ignatius de Loyola was a former Spanish soldier, whose leg had been smashed by a cannonball during the defense of the northern city of Pamplona, when he and five followers founded the Jesuit Order in 1534. The new and highly disciplined arm of the Church received papal approval in 1540. By the time of Loyola's death in 1556 there were 100 Jesuit colleges and energetic missionaries could be found from Mexico to the doors of China. The Jesuits turned back the Protestant tide and recaptured for Catholicism much of Germany, most of Hungary and Bohemia, and all of Christian Poland. It is difficult to find in history another group so small that accomplished so much in such a short time.

## Does the Pope Own the Papal States?

As a result of the eager and energetic scholarship of Renaissance humanists and their study of classical Latin, many previous assumptions as well as revered documents were proven invalid. One of the most glaring examples came in the fifteenth century, a result of the philological study of Lorenzo Valla (c. 1407–1457). He proved conclusively that an early fourth-century document, in which Emperor Constantine (d. 337) granted spiritual primacy in the west and temporal rule of the papal states (central Italy) to the Roman popes, was in fact a fabrication. He showed that certain terms within the text had never been a part of ancient Latin, but rather came into use no earlier than the eighth century. The feudal term *fief* was a certain giveaway. While this discovery might appear to have been a challenge to papal authority, it was none other than Pope Nicholas V who founded the Vatican Library and made Valla his secretary. As Martin Luther would discover, popes loved the secular side of humanism.

# Religious Hatred and Commerce in the Far East

Those who have read *Shogun* by James Clavell or seen the mini-series on television were no doubt struck by the ferocious animosity between Protestant and Catholic European visitors in Japanese lands. The friction was even greater if the parties involved were Calvinists (i.e., Dutch) and Jesuits or their adherents. Clavell was most accurate in his historical understanding and treatment of this phenomenon. The religious hatreds of the Reformation era had simply been transferred to another geographical location. Ironically, Dutch Calvinist merchants had an advantage in establishing Japanese depots for trade, as they would readily submit to a test employed by the Japanese to prove that they were not as bad as those other "foreign devils." All they had to do was publicly trample on a crucifix. This was not an onerous task for those who believed that most of the images and rituals essential to Catholicism amounted to nothing better than flagrant idolatry, which the Calvinists derisively called "Romanism" or "Popery."

# CHAPTER IV

# The Seventeenth Century

The century that opened with the death of the great Queen Elizabeth I (1603) and the waning era of Shakespeare brought the Stuart dynasty to the English scene, saw the convulsions of civil war and the Puritan rule of Oliver Cromwell at mid-century, then witnessed the restoration of the Stuarts, and closed with the Glorious Revolution of 1688. Expanding world trade featured competition among British, Dutch, and French interests. The seeds that would grow to form the new United States by 1783 were planted during this century, and many of the liberties and rights associated with British traditions were won by Englishmen (hence also Americans) during the struggle between royal and parliamentary forces. The European continent witnessed the final round in the four phases of the great religious wars, which led to the peace of Westphalia in 1648 and the economic exhaustion of the Germanies. In France, the skillful political touch of the famous Cardinal Richelieu shaped and cemented the absolute monarchy. By 1660 Louis XIV, the Grand Monarch, and his *Belle France* had moved to dominate the European scene, a position the country would hold for five decades. The Palace of Versailles set the standards for the rest of Europe in politics, drama, music, and society. From his capital Louis waged four long wars in search of "natural frontiers" for France, including battles for the Rhine, the Bay of Biscay, and the Pyrenees. These wars ultimately exhausted the French economy, enhancing the positions of both Austria and Prussia and making England the dominant economic power on the seas of the world.

## Questions for Discussion

- Is the question of Queen Elizabeth's virginity irrelevant? Why? What was Queen Elizabeth's greatest love? How do we know?

- What is unique about the beginning of the first phase of the Thirty Years' War?

- Were people of standing concerned with style and manners during the age of Louis XIV?

- Is there any evidence that Louis XIV had a larger than normal stomach? Were his doctors any better prepared or equipped to deal with illness than were King Charles II's doctors in England?

- What does the case of William Prynne indicate about the severity of punishments in the seventeenth century? Can such punishments be attributed to the religious or social nature of the society? What effect did the religious and social views of England have on the civil war (1642–1649) between Puritans and the forces of Charles II? Prynne was tried and sentenced by the Star Chamber. Do you think this has any bearing on the dissolution of the Star Chamber by Parliament after the civil war?

# Characteristics of European Society

The dawn of the seventeenth century revealed little progress in morals, manners, or customs. Much of the knowledge about these social customs comes from the criticisms of the more sober Protestants (especially Calvinists on both sides of the English Channel) and from laws whose prohibitive contents indicate the nature of crimes and the social climate. Some examples follow.

## Prostitution

Prostitution was widespread among all classes, with separate names for the practicers depending upon their clientele. Louis XIII (1610–1643) issued an ordinance (1635) directing that all proven prostitutes be whipped, shaved, and banished, and that all pimps or solicitors be sent to the galleys for life. Yet there is little evidence of any solid enforcement. Montaigne in his *Essays* refers to perversions of various types and a change of sex by a woman of 22, and other sources indicate that print-shop windows afforded citizens ready displays of erotic pictures and printed materials.

## Duels

The sword became a common part of male dress, apparently contributing to an increasing number of private duels. Duels were strictly forbidden, but Montaigne even described mini-battles that resulted from the expectation that seconds and thirds also fight. Later, Cardinal Richelieu's edict against dueling was rigidly enforced until his death in 1642.

## Prison Life

For one of wealth and position, a prison term in the Bastille might be sumptuous and comfortable (at the prisoner's expense), but a commoner (95 percent of society) faced insufferable dangers, banishment to desolate colonies, or the galleys. In the latter case, "G A L" was branded on the prisoner's back, a fate experienced by many a Protestant captured during the religious wars. It is evident that crime was frequent; robbery, murder, and danger to life and limb were regular; and, of course, punishments were harsh.

## Manners and Society

For the royal court and the wealthy, dress was lavish, decorative, and extravagant for both sexes, but this did not deter the finest from eating with their fingers at an elegant dinner. The use of forks only began to spread after 1600. Wine and beer were the favored drinks, largely due to the dangerous quality of water (James I of England resented having to use it even for bathing), but coffee and chocolate had made their appearance by the beginning of the seventeenth century. Some physicians believed chocolate caused diarrhea, and memoirist Mme. de Sévigné told the story of a pregnant lady who consumed chocolate to such excess that she gave birth to "a little boy black as the devil" (author's translation). All classes enjoyed dancing of some fashion; the royal court especially liked expensive, costume balls and playing tennis.

# Elizabeth I:
# The Virgin Queen?

Probably the most questioned aspect of England's great queen is that of her virginity, a question that concentrates on two issues: Was she in fact a virgin and, if so, for what reasons did she remain so? (Historians have never agreed upon either issue, and there is no reason to believe that any new evidence will surface to provide precise and accurate answers.)

From contemporaries, there is much that falls into the category of gossip: that she had a "membrane on her that made her incapable of man"; that a physician persuaded her to avoid attempts at bearing children because she had certain physical defects (as expressed by sixteenth-century English antiquarian William Camden in his *Annales*); or that she was herself aware that she could not bear children owing to defects that had resulted from her father's (Henry VIII's) syphilis, a view much accepted because of the difficulties suffered by Catherine of Aragon, half-sister Mary, and half-brother Edward VI.

Historian J. A. Froude (*History of England from the Fall of Wolsey to the Defeat of the Spanish Armada*) asserts that despite Queen Elizabeth's love for Lord Robert Dudley—whom she titled and did much to enrich, and with whom she shared more private company than any other—"nothing unseemly" ever passed between them. But the queen's relationship with Lord Dudley does support the view that in all things England came first for her, that England was always her first love, and that no conduct on her part must serve to blemish that cardinal love. Dudley was married to Amy Robsart, but was not living with her. He was residing at Windsor with Elizabeth when Amy fell down a flight of stairs and broke her neck in an "accident" that took her life.

There were indeed rumors, which historians generally consider unfounded, but the net result was that Elizabeth ended her personal relationship with Dudley and eventually offered him as a prospective husband to Mary, Queen of Scots. As always, England came first for Elizabeth, an attitude expressed in her often-used reply to compliments or flattery from foreign ambassadors: "I'm merely English."

# Henry Establishes the Bourbon Dynasty

Henry IV (1586–1610) is looked upon by his country as the first modern king of France. His victories over the extreme Catholic party led by the House of Guise ended a half century of brutal religious wars, and his personal acceptance of Catholicism, a compromise to bring peace, permitted his entry into Paris without a long siege. He subsequently issued an edict of toleration at Nantes that provided security and freedom of worship to the Protestant minority. With the aid of his talented minister, Sully, he gave France solid and forward-looking administration until he was struck down by the dagger of a Catholic fanatic named François Ravaillac. Put to torture the assassin confessed all, but insisted he had acted in the cause of righteousness.

On the personal side, Henry exhibited the morals of many a Renaissance ruler. In his biography of the king, H. D. Sedgewick describes a man seasoned by years of military campaigning, with the bearing, morals, and odor of a soldier. He was likely to organize a hunt after an all-day march, and to his last years demonstrated consistent courage despite suffering from dysentery, gout, and diarrhea. One friend said that he usually "stank like a corpse." This did not seem to hamper his love life, for he engaged a retinue of delightful mistresses quite undeterred, even by gonorrhea. Ultimately a divorce from wife Margot was arranged, not so he could marry one of his mistresses, but rather for political reasons, so Henry could marry Maria, scion of the de Medici banking family of Florence. This marriage cancelled a large debt owed by France. The king rushed to greet his new wife at Lyons, provided her with all the courtesies of royalty, and, once she was pregnant with the future Louis XIII, returned to the arms of his current mistress. Ultimately Maria de Medici bore Henry seven children in ten years, and he had them all raised together with his royal bastards.

# How the Thirty Years' War Began

Bohemian leaders in Prague wished to rule their province with local autonomy, without the interference of the Holy Roman

Emperor. When, after heated argument, the imperial commissioners in Prague insisted that the Bohemians respect the Emperor's authority, the Bohemian leaders bodily threw the said agents from a third-story window. The agents were not physically injured, for they landed in some large piles of manure that were awaiting spreading. This incident is known as the "defenestration of Prague"; in German, the word for window is *das Fenster.*

## Ravages of the Thirty Years' War

The last of the great religious wars of the Reformation era set the Germanies back 50 years in terms of social and economic development, according to conservative historical estimates. This third of the four phases of the religious wars pitted the marauding armies of Sweden's Gustavus Adolphus (Lutheran) against the equally mobile and destructive forces of Emperor Maximilian's (Catholic) generals. The former were well financed by a prince of the Catholic Church, Cardinal Richelieu of France, the latter, of course, by Pope Urban VIII.

War does make for strange bedfellows, just as politics does, hence deceiving the party seeking genuine religious motives. For example, for the Catholic cause General Tilly, at Neubrandenburg, slaughtered the garrison of 3,000 men, while a month later the Protestant cause was enhanced when Gustavus took Frankfurt-an-der-Oder and slaughtered the garrison of 2,000 men. Tilly and his forces then laid siege to Magdeburg, which held out for six months before the Catholic troops finally entered and plundered for four days, slaughtering 3,000 garrison soldiers and 17,000 of the town's 36,000 inhabitants. All but the cathedral was burned. This was followed by a great victory for combined Protestant forces under Gustavus at Breitenfeld. Emperor Maximilian sought new armies, and in 1632 one of the greatest matches of the war found the two best generals of the age face to face at Lutzen—Gustavus, the Lion of the North, against the Catholic forces of Count Wallenstein; 25,000 Protestants versus 40,000 Catholics. The lines wavered and re-formed all day in bloody hand-to-hand combat; and when it appeared that his center was giving way to the opposing forces, Gustavus personally led a wild cavalry charge into the midst of enemy lines. The Swedish ruler's biographer, C. Fletcher, reports that Gustavus suffered shots in the arm and back and was unhorsed before enemy soldiers surrounded him and asked who he was. He answered, "I'm the King of Sweden, who does seal the religion and liberty of the German nation in my blood." All took their turn at what became a Protestant pincushion for their swords. Angered, the Swedes rallied under able lieutenants and claimed a costly victory. Though the body of their leader was retrieved and his memory avenged, that night the victors could not bring themselves to celebrate.

After this final phase of the war many parts of Germany and Austria were as desolate as they had been in the period immediately after the ravages of the fourteenth-century Great Plague. Moderate estimates calculate a drop in population from 22 million to less than 14 million. Many villages were deserted and not reoccupied for years, while houses were destroyed wherever the war had reached, fields remained fallow, and hunger stalked some regions in such savage degrees that steps had to be taken to prevent cannibalism (C. V. Wedgwood, *The Thirty Years' War*).

# Restoration Styles: The Puritan Pressure Lifted

For many, the removal of the Puritan elements associated with the Cromwellian (1645–1660) era from the seats of power made it seem as though a fresh wind had swept over England. Save for the Puritans and Quakers, language again became openly profane in print and speech and on the stage. Theaters reopened and the use of powdered wigs expanded widely among those who could afford them, for as Samuel Pepys relates in his diary, the wearing of a powdered wig required a shaved head and regular maintenance of the wig. Men again dressed fashionably and expensively, with the requisite dangling sword.

Women who could afford to be fashionable also made use of false hair, which was often supported by hidden wires and curled into ringlets. A trend later satirized in France by Montesquieu was that of applying black spots or patches here and there on the face or exposed parts of the body, as if to draw special attention to that location. Shoulders and breasts gained greater exposure, while the quantity of makeup used by some women caused Professor Walter Besant of London to take seriously a play in which a woman at day's end disassembled herself into 20 boxes, and then at noon the next day reassembled all the parts, like a great German clock.

# The Agony of Death for England's Charles II

The third Stuart ruler of England (1660–1685) is known to history as the "Merry Monarch," for he presided over the relaxation of the rigid standards that had been enforced by Puritan leaders, was handsome and indulgent, and delighted the gossip-mongers by running through a string of mistresses, the best known of whom was Nell Gwyn. However, the story of his last days offers a picture of physical torment and suffering that his physicians appear to have aggravated rather than alleviated.

The first in the series of events that led to his demise was a convulsion that left his face distorted and his mouth foaming, after which his doctors bled him and stabilized his condition. For five days a team of eighteen physicians treated him. Then, as described by medical historian C. E. Turner, they again tapped his veins, applied cupping glasses to his shoulders, cut off his hair to raise blisters on the scalp, and treated the soles of his feet with plasters of pigeon dung. To clear his head they forced herbs up his nostrils to induce sneezing, forced him to drink antimony and sulfate so he would vomit to clear his stomach, and cleared his bowels with a combination of laxatives and enemas.

He grew worse, and though in formal practice he was a Protestant, he accepted the Catholic priest offered by his brother for last rites, requested pardons for friends and enemies, asked in his wife's presence that his latest mistress (Louise Keroualle) and bastard children receive proper care, and apologized for taking so long to die. Historian Thomas Macaulay reports his last words as, "Let not poor Nelly starve."

## Louis XIV, the Grand Monarch

Though deprived as a youth, only occasionally given tattered garments and provided with ill-supervised education and training, Louis XIV (1661–1714) became a king who set standards for all Europe in sumptuousness and style. The following observations are representative of the lifestyle of France's "Sun King."

Between the time he arose at 8:00 A.M. and mass an hour later he was attended by more than a dozen servants and observed by those rewarded with a chance to see him take morning wine, don the first of several wigs for the day, or sprinkle himself with powder. He was shaved on alternate days.

Louis was a champion eater at his two meals a day, and an autopsy revealed a stomach capacity twice the normal size for humans. The princess Palatine reported having observed the royal master devour four bowls of assorted soups, one whole pheasant, a partridge, a large dish of salad, two large slices of ham, mutton cooked in gravy with garlic, and a plate of pastries, all followed by fruit and hard-boiled eggs. That would suffice until the late dinner around 10:00 P.M., a meal of greater size and variety. When Louis retired for the night there was placed beside his bed a roasted chicken, two loaves of bread, and two bottles of wine.

Louis's personal physician, Valot, prescribed regular bleeding for the king, at first and last quarters of the moon, when his "humours" would have returned to the center of his body, and a purgative soup was used to flush the bowels that once caused the king to visit the toilet eleven times in an eight-hour period. Valot's successor, Daquin, preferred to use Arabic prescriptions on his master, which included earthworms to cure gout, bees' ashes to make hair grow, and ant-oil to ward off deafness.

## "Rock-a-Bye Baby" and the Glorious Revolution

The crucial development that brought English parliamentary and military leaders to invite a foreign ruler's forces to join them in overthrowing their own King James II (1685–1688) was the birth of a male royal heir in June of 1688. James was a known Catholic activist in a nation predominantly Protestant, and he proved to all concerned that they could not wait for geriatrics to remove the problem. Interesting rumors spread through Protestant London regarding the circumstances of the child's birth, and these rumors became the origin of a well-known lullaby.

The rumors suggested that the queen had not actually become pregnant, but instead had been secluded from all but Jesuits and Catholic aides to await the arrival of a child who would be delivered at the proper time in a warming pan; premature announcement of the birth merely added credence to the rumors.

As tradition has it, a little song of anonymous origin came to be heard around the streets and among all age groups, alluding to this sinister Catholic plot to provide an heir to the throne: "Rock-a-bye baby, in the tree tops, when the wind blows the cradle will rock [as more people become aware, the pressure on the conspirators will increase], when the bough breaks [the plot is exposed], the cradle will fall, and down will come baby, cradle and all [the downfall of the king and the clique of Catholic supporters]."

# Puritan Rectitude:
# The Punishment of William Prynne

By the early seventeenth century fanatical Puritans had become highly vocal in their attacks on the scandalous character of English theater. One of their most vehement spokesmen was a lawyer named William Prynne, who wrote, published, and widely circulated a scurrilous attack called *Histrio-Mastix, the Players Scourge*. He not only charged that most plays were obscene and wanton (most were), but he also, although quite eloquently, called the actresses whores. It so happened that Queen Harrietta Maria had just imported actresses from France, and was herself rehearsing for a part in a court masque. Even though Prynne apologized to the queen, William Laud, Archbishop of Canterbury, had the verbose Puritan indicted for seditious libel.

Subsequently, Prynne was debarred from the practice of law, sentenced to life imprisonment, placed for a time in pillory, and had both his ears cut off. From prison he issued *News From Ipswich*, in which he denounced Anglican prelates as devilish traitors and ravenous wolves and recommended that all such vermin be hanged. He was pilloried again, and the stumps of his ears were torn away. He remained in jail until the Long Parliament freed him four years later, in 1640.

# CHAPTER V

# The Eighteenth Century

Owing to the temper of the great minds of the contemporary European scene, the eighteenth century has often been referred to as the Age of Urbanity. Much of the most studied literature concentrated upon heavy topics such as law, government, toleration, prejudice, liberties, rights, equality, or the conduct of humans toward fellow humans and the universe (Isaac Newton died in 1727). Europeans dominated commerce, and colonies expanded around the world. Meanwhile, Prussia, Russia, and Austria expanded their power and size at the expense of Poland, Sweden, and Ottoman Turkey. England firmly established herself as the supreme naval power, and conditions in France by the end of the century provoked the first great modern political and social revolution. The fury spilled over France's borders, and soon involved most of Europe. The subsequent series of wars produced a new empire in the hands of Napoleon Bonaparte that cast its hegemony across all of Europe, with the exception of England.

Developments in America included the Great Awakening, Queen Anne's War, King George's War, and the French and Indian War. The second half of the century witnessed the careers of such illustrious American colonial leaders as Benjamin Franklin, George Washington, Thomas Jefferson, the Adams family, and others who forged a new nation by 1787.

## Questions for Discussion

- Did women of means take special care of their physical appearance in the eighteenth century? Were games popular? Was this an age of romantic love? Were there any changes in moral standards from the previous century?

- Why was one war called the War of Jenkins' Ear? Is it possible that there was still some religious animosity between England and Spain?

- How was Frederick the Great as a young man taught a lesson in responsibility?

- What is King Louis XV of France best known for? Did he earn the label as the laziest king of France? How?

- Why might important persons in politics and diplomacy on both sides of the English Channel after 1760 have known about the Chevalier D'Eon? Would such an individual create as much comment today in modern politics?

- The French Revolution brought with it what new and unique method for execution? Was this method used for political or criminal offenders?

- What does the episode of Charlotte Corday and Jean-Paul Marat tell us about the fever of the French revolutionary era? Would you characterize Charlotte Corday as a woman of serious political dedication with a strong sense of national duty? Why?

- When the name Napoleon is introduced, most listeners are likely to think of battles, victories, and the glory of France. What type of person was Napoleon? Did he love Josephine? Was he hardworking? How did he conduct himself? How did his only natural son come to rest next to him in one of the most visited shrines in all of Paris? What is the speculation surrounding his death? What attributes did he demonstrate as an administrator and as head of a family? What were the reasons for his divorce from Josephine?

## Samuel Johnson's London

By the middle of the eighteenth century London was an overgrown metropolitan morass of 725,000 souls. It was filled daily with the noises of coaches, beggars, hawkers, organ-grinders, barking dogs, and the clattering of horses' hooves on the cobblestone streets. Many streets were dangerous, even at high noon; more than 50,000 prostitutes plied their trade in competition with pickpockets and thieves. Samuel Johnson, commenting on the condition of prison life, calculated that of the 20,000 bankrupts imprisoned in an average year, 5,000 died of privation within 12 months. He also argued that making the death penalty mandatory for robbery and for murder would encourage criminals to conceal the first by committing the second.

## The Commonplace Use of Tobacco and Gin

The use of snuff (fine powdered tobacco) had become common among both sexes and was widely believed to have medical benefits—the sneezing it caused would clear nasal passages; it could cure headaches, colds, deafness, and sleepiness; it soothed nerves; and it generally improved brain functioning. Hence the snuffbox was part of the wardrobe of any man or woman who dressed in style. The author Henry Fielding saw gin as one of the chief evils that was poisoning the lower classes, many of whom took it as wages, drinking two pints daily and often consuming little else.

## Criticism of University Life

Some of England's better minds of the eighteenth century believed that university education was at a low ebb. Lord Chesterfield described Cambridge as "sunk into the lowest obscurity." Oxford appeared devoted to the standards and attitudes of the previous century. Adam Smith, the author of *The Wealth of Nations*, said he learned nothing at Oxford, while Edward Gibbon denounced its dons as ignorant boozers and regretted the years he wasted at the university.

## Enhancing the Feminine Mystique

Stylish women of the eighteenth century began to wear reinforced hairdos so lofty that their hair had to be guarded against being ignited by chandeliers. In his *Persian Letters*, Montesquieu tells that women's hairstyles became so high that the tops of doorways had to be raised and that, in perspective, it appeared that a woman's face was in her middle. Artificial beauty patches were placed on women's faces or bosoms whenever a little extra attention was desired.

## Manners and Customs of the Comfortable

As it was unwise to be out at night in Paris or London, most people of means entertained themselves at home with drink, music, conversation, chess, draughts (American checkers), billiards, and cards. Even evangelical parsons played at something, and in 1742 Edmond Hoyle systematized the laws of whist (bridge), giving rise to the phrase "according to Hoyle."

## Managed Marriages

In France, marrying without parental consent was on the increase in literature but seldom occurred in reality, even at the peasant level. Family units and property control were much too important. The legal age of marriage was 14 for boys and 13 for girls, but children could be betrothed at age 7, the age that medieval philosophy called the "age of reason." Because property and title were of such significance, the man might be as much as 40 years older than his wife. The Marquise de Sauveboeuf was already a widow at 13.

## Morals of the Upper Class: A Double Standard

For the aristocracy, there was no social stigma attached to adultery. The general view held that such action was an acceptable and pleasant substitute for divorce, since the national religion (Catholicism) forbade divorce. A husband leaving for diplomatic or military duty might logically take along his mistress with no need for explanation or secrecy. That is why Montesquieu, in his

*Persian Letters,* wrote that, in France, "a husband who would wish to have sole possession of his wife would be regarded as a disturber of the public happiness, and as a fool who should wish to enjoy the light of the sun to the exclusion of other men." He added that a Frenchman never talked about his wife behind her back, for it was always possible that those to whom he was speaking knew his wife better than he did.

# Two Examples of Economic Expansion

The wars of Louis XIV and the great wars of eighteenth-century imperial rivalry, in all of which England and France were on opposite sides regardless of the other alignments, also had an economic feature in either provocation or results. The expansion of European nationalistic interests took on a worldwide character, of which commerce on the high seas became an essential feature. The mushrooming wealth in trade has been related by historian R. R. Palmer in his *History of the Modern World* through two examples.

## The Making of the Pitt Fortune

Thomas Pitt, an individual from a poor and simple family, went to India in 1674, where he engaged in illegal trade in competition with the East India Company, a firm that held an accepted British monopoly for specified geographical areas and commodities. A century later, the American Boston Tea Party was an attack against this monopoly and the company as well. Upon his return to England, Pitt was financially capable of paying a fine equivalent to $20,000 and purchasing the manor of Stratford, a property that included the borough of Old Sarum and hence a seat in the House of Commons. When he returned to India, his talents were so valued that he was able to trade independently as well as serve the East India Company. In 1704 he purchased a 410-carat uncut diamond for just over the equivalent of $1 million. Back in Europe, Pitt had the diamond cut by experts in Amsterdam and later sold it to the regent of France, in 1717, for approximately $3,375,000.

Wealth opened doors in England more readily than on the Continent. One of Thomas Pitt's daughters became the countess of Stanhope and one of his sons became the earl of Londonderry. Another son gained a seat in the House of Lords as the earl of Chatham and was the father of William Pitt, who as prime minister was the architect of British global victories in the Seven Years' War (also known as the French and Indian War) with France. It was after William Pitt that a fort, which later became a prominent city in Pennsylvania, was named, a perfect example of how wealth earned in one area of the world came to influence politics in London and expansion of the frontiers of North America. The earl of Chatham's second son, William Pitt the Younger, became British prime minister at the age of 24 and was the chief policymaker facing the threat of Napoleon until his death in 1806.

## The Accomplishments of Jean-Joseph Laborde

Born to a modest middle-class family in southern France, Jean-Joseph Laborde went to work for relatives in the 1740s in the port city of Bayonne, engaging in commerce both east and west. He soon became an entrepreneur, a plantation owner, and a slave trader in the Caribbean. He amassed a fortune through sugar imports and the supply of manufactured goods to colonial plantations. His extensive investments soon made him one of the most prominent bankers in Paris. His daughter became a countess, and he was awarded the title of marquis. As a real estate magnate, he was responsible for large suburban development in Paris, and during the Seven Years' War he was sent as special envoy to Spain to ask for loans to support French war efforts. Interestingly, Spanish authorities flatly refused any loans to France's Louis XV but at the same time indicated willingness to loan Laborde 20 million reals. For the French war effort on behalf of American independence, he raised $15 million for his government and hence contributed to the founding of a new republic on the western side of the Atlantic. He gave approximately $30,000 annually to charity and in a single year (1788) raised $500,000 for hospital construction in Paris. In 1789 his funds were used to help finance the insurrection that led to the storming of the Bastille, which began the French Revolution. Although one of his sons was an active participant in revolutionary activities such as the famous Tennis Court Oath, Laborde himself was guillotined in 1794. We all know the saying of how a revolution often "devours its own children."

## The Severed Ear of Captain Jenkins

By 1738 Robert Walpole had headed the English Cabinet for nearly two decades; a hallmark of his administration had been peace and conciliation abroad. Many disgruntled members of Parliament, however, viewed his policy as peace at any price. As British commerce continued to expand, it brought more frequent friction and altercations with Spain and Spanish colonies, where Spain wished to retain a monopoly. Walpole's opponents drew harrowing pictures during parliamentary debates, charging that English sailors were rotting in Spanish jails and English captains and crews were abused and mistreated by coastal patrols along American shores and on the high seas.

Finally, to prove their point, they resorted to physical evidence. They brought to Parliament Captain Robert Jenkins, who carried a small box that contained, on a bed of cotton, his shriveled ear. It had been cut off by a Spanish cutlass when his ship had been stopped while sailing in Spanish waters. To add insult to injury, the Spanish captain had threatened to do the same to King George II himself, should he ever intrude into Spanish waters. The war that soon resulted, largely a commercial struggle confined to the high seas, is known to students of English history as the War of Jenkins' Ear.

## Peter the Great: Born To Roister

Tsar of Russia at the beginning of the eighteenth century, Peter the Great (1682–1725) founded the new capital at St. Petersburg, introduced science, technology, and many western advances into his country, successfully concluded a long struggle with Sweden over Russia's western provinces, and westernized the royal court by forcing men to shave their beards, shorten their robes, and accept women into the routine of court life. No historian doubts Peter's claim as a hard-working ruler, but his methods of relaxation have often drawn greater attention.

Before he was 20, Peter proved himself an accomplished drinker. Visits to the German quarter of Moscow, and gatherings that he hosted, usually ended in drunken revels. He found particular delight in forcing some young girl who could not keep up with him to drain a huge glass of vodka without removing it from her lips. Always something of a jester and a drunkard, Peter gave full rein to excess of every kind when he organized the "drunken Council of Fools." He personally drafted a ritual for the group and its drunken sessions (or spectacles). Consistent with his mockery of the hierarchy of organized religion (both Eastern Orthodox and Roman Catholic), he named his former tutor the pope-patriarch of the group, and then dedicated the council ceremonies to Venus and Bacchus. The residence of this pope-patriarch was called the Vatican, where His Holiness was served by a group of stutterers dressed as Catholic cardinals and sat on a throne made of wine casks and decorated with bottles. There was even a mock election (i.e., College of Cardinals) of a new pope-patriarch, which was celebrated with a parade in which the newly elected official rode on a wine vat drawn by four oxen, preceded by Peter, who was dressed as a sailor and beating on a drum. They were attended by dwarfs dressed as monks and followed by a train of assorted carts pulled by goats, pigs, bears, and reindeer. A relative giant, Peter was six feet nine inches tall in an age when the average height was probably five feet six inches. Dwarfs and midgets fascinated him, and he loved to cavort with them whenever the opportunity arose.

Peter also appreciated lewdness and cruelty. He enjoyed the filthiest of jokes and comical interjections into serious events such as funerals. He was delighted by punishments such as flogging, impaling, roasting, and especially beard-burning. He loved firework displays, and was amused when a rocket discharge decapitated a curious onlooker.

He had several mistresses, and made one of them his tsarina. All in all, he was a man of sharp and extreme contrasts who is colorfully described by Melvin C. Wren in his *The Course of Russian History*.

## Frederick the Great

For most casual students of history the name Frederick the Great (ruled 1740–1786) brings to mind themes similarly associated with

Alexander or Charles the Great—military campaigns and success on the battlefield. That would be a reaction both logical and historically accurate, for Frederick's small Hohenzollern state was locked in struggle with the forces of one or more European states on several occasions. Frederick proved to be the most capable commander and tactician of the second half of the seventeenth century. However, he is the same person who, while only the young heir to the throne, attempted to unlock the wonders of the world by running away to England with a friend. His punishment for the failed attempt, personally prescribed by his father, was the forced personal observation of his best friend's execution. He was indeed one who as an adult and ruler of a model Germanic Prussian state used only German in the barracks and for command. However, he composed music and (always in French) wrote poetry and conversed on weighty topics. He played the flute and invited the best of scholars, intellectuals, and artists to his palace near Potsdam, a palace he named Sans Souci (without care). Even when aroused with anger by news of the alliance against him Elizabeth Petrovna of Russia had arranged with France, he resorted to the cultural tongue of the century and publicly called her *catin du nord* (slut from the north).

## The Wit of Voltaire

It is not unusual that a student, impressed and inspired by his admired mentor, will attempt to outdo his mentor in thought and deed. One such lad, greatly influenced by what he judged as Voltaire's iconoclastic zeal, declared loudly that all religions were merely human fabrications and that any bright and reasonable person was capable of starting his or her own religion; the youth indicated his intent to forthwith start his own religion. When he solicited Voltaire's advice regarding this project, the scholar suggested that the young man go out and have himself killed and then "rise on the third day."

By the time he was 30, Voltaire had already combined fame and fortune. He was recognized by most as France's greatest living poet, and circulated freely both at the royal court and in most areas of elite society. Some among the highborn, however, resented the intrusion of this bourgeois upstart into the best of salons, the opera, and court functions. One such person was the scion of a family whose prestige dated from the age of Saint Louis, a man who had served the crown in numerous positions and who could count even the rank of cardinal on the limbs of his family tree. The incident that grew out of an attempt by this man, Chevalier de Rohan-Chabot, to embarrass Voltaire in front of other notables has been related variously by those who observed it (including biographer Georg Brandes), but there is no doubt that the incident occurred. Let us take the account of the meeting in the lobby of the Comédie-Française, in December of 1725 (loosely translated): Rohan-Chabot (after all his titles have been listed by way of introduction): "Voltaire, Voltaire, I have never heard that name." Voltaire: "That is because I am the first of my line and you are the tail end of yours."

Six weeks later Voltaire was lunching at the house of the Duc de Sully and was summoned to the front gate to receive a message. There, six ruffians pounced on him and beat him while Rohan-Chabot looked on from his coach, cautioning his thugs to avoid hitting the writer's head in case something good eventually came out of it. Voltaire's later attempt, after training, to engage the chevalier in a duel was thwarted by the former's arrest and incarceration in the Bastille.

## Louis XV: France's Laziest King

Monarchs are often associated with or remembered for particular aspects or events of their reign. For example, Louis XIII, though quite lazy in his own right, is better known to history because of his able minister Cardinal Richelieu and the popularity of the Dumas novel *The Three Musketeers*. Louis XV (1714–1772) is best known for a chain of famous mistresses, the most remembered and by far the most influential being Madame de Pompadour. The reason for her great influence over the king, and hence in political affairs, was simple: When she was no longer the mistress of the royal bed, she filled the role of recruiting, evaluating, screening, and preparing new mistresses. This was a delicate but important role. An indication of her power was the resentment felt toward her by the Prussian king Frederick the Great, who referred to her by the family name of her common background, before she was "discovered" and titled by Louis: Madame Poisson (which means fish).

Louis XV may indeed have been France's laziest monarch. He spent much of his time on the hobby that was his second obsession (after mistresses): tinkering with clocks. And in another of his amusements we find a unique example of sloth. When he hunted, rather than cautiously moving through the forest in search of his quarry, Louis merely had peasants drive deer past his lodge, and he shot at the animals from an upstairs window.

# Madame de Pompadour: Mistress of Louis XV

The most famous mistress of all eighteenth-century European courts was certainly Jeanne Antoinette Poisson, the Marquise de Pompadour. She had beauty, grace, compassion, a brilliant mind, a congenial personality, and strength of will. She was for more than a decade a force in governmental decisions. Talented in the techniques of diplomacy, she was a protector of Voltaire and Diderot and a confidante of *philosophes.* Some additional facts about her are also of interest.

1. Rather than referring to her by the title bestowed by Louis XV, the dauphin (son of Louis and heir to the throne) insisted on calling her Madame Whore. He, however, tolerated her, which the court clergy refused to do.

2. She had a personal library of 3,500 volumes and had a profound influence in elevating France to a position of European cultural leadership.

3. The Jesuits successfully advised that the king's confessor withhold the sacraments from him as long as his mistress remained at the royal court. Even when her sexual relations with the king had ended and she took to regular and devoted religious worship, the confessor did not relent until Madame de Pompadour remarried.

4. When she no longer shared the king's bed she became the official procurer, screener, and trainer of new mistresses for the king, employing a cottage on a far corner of the grounds at Versailles. Later Louis accorded her the status of duchess, and gave her the

post of *dame du palais de la reine* (regal lady of the court). This position required that she reside at the court; the Jesuits withdrew their expulsion demands, and she was allowed to participate in the sacraments.

5. There was never anyone whose company, conversation, ideas, charm, and wit Louis enjoyed more, so Madame de Pompadour was always more than just a mistress. In 1756 she was instrumental in the formation of a marriage alliance with Austria (the daughter of Maria Theresa, Marie Antoinette, was betrothed to the future Louis XVI) against Prussia, which provoked Frederick the Great to change his nickname for her from Madame Fish to merely "Petticoat Four at the French court."

# The Diplomat Chevalier d'Eon: Male or Female?

D'Eon de Beaumont served France for some 40 years in various diplomatic capacities and helped negotiate the Treaty of 1763 at the close of the Seven Years' War. Shortly thereafter, however, questions arose about his sex, questions that are still not conclusively settled. Contention about his sexual identity even led to betting, with wagers reaching many thousands of pounds among English gentlemen. Insurance agents soon covered bets with contracts that were legally enforceable, and fears grew that as a result the chevalier might be kidnapped. In the meantime, according to historian Janet Burke in her study of women in the freemasonry of France, the diplomat rose to the ranks of third degree in the Masonic order.

The upshot was a trial at which a doctor and a journalist both testified, on the basis of personal experience, that d'Eon was in fact a woman, and the jury agreed. The chevalier then made an open declaration to the French ministers that he was a woman. The declaration coincided with negotiations with the French government, which agreed to pay d'Eon a lifetime pension if he agreed from that time forward to wear only female garments. He then returned to France as the Chevalière d'Eon and appeared only in female dress until his death in 1810. An autopsy performed at that time, verified by two of France's most respected surgeons, stated that the deceased had been of the male sex.

## The Repeated Appearance
## of Boswell's Clap

The foregoing represents not only a statement of a condition but also the title of an article by medical historian William B. Ober (*And Other Essays*, Southern Illinois University Press, 1979). Long known to history, primarily for his *Life of Samuel Johnson*, James Boswell's (1740–1795) personal life as revealed in his own journals and diaries was not uncovered for twentieth-century readers until his papers were discovered in Scottish and Irish castles and then edited by scholars at Yale University. These diaries reveal that Boswell contracted no fewer than 12 gonorrheal infections between the ages of 20 and 50, as well as suffering intermittent attacks of the symptoms for long periods in between developing new infections. That may indeed represent some sort of a record, but we must keep in mind that the state of medicine and protection was not then what it is today.

The diaries also reveal the psychological torment of a man of Presbyterian upbringing with a full consciousness of sin; a man who condemned prostitutes and brothels in his writings, but who could not resist his periodic temptation to visit them. He employed alcohol to reduce inhibitions until his sexual appetites had been sated. In the midst of all of this, Boswell married and his wife had nine pregnancies, from which three daughters and two sons survived to maturity. There is no evidence that his wife, Margaret, ever suffered from symptoms associated with gonorrhea.

## The Guillotine: Humanitarian
## and Democratic Instrument

In 1789 Joseph-Ignace Guillotin was elected to the French National Assembly, a body that would soon after become the central sounding board of the revolution. As a member of this body (which by 1792 was called the Legislative Assembly), he sponsored a law requiring that all death sentences be carried out by "means of a machine." The rationale was twofold: No longer would beheading be reserved only to persons of noble birth; and the specified technique would be as painless as possible. At first called the Louisette, the machine soon took on the name of the legislator and we have known it since as the guillotine.

During the revolution and for some years afterward it was often called the "French national barber," and in the twentieth century criminals referred to it as "the window." Yet the guillotine was a rather humanitarian invention, since it replaced the block and axe, a method that could become messy if the executioner did not sever the head with a single blow and the second swing did not hit in the same spot. In recent times the machine has been used sparingly, the last occasion being in 1977. The French government outlawed capital punishment in 1981, leaving the guillotine to serve as a museum piece.

## The Proud Marie Antoinette

In October of 1793 Queen Marie Antoinette, nearly eight months after her husband's execution, was tried before the Revolutionary Tribunal, with Fouquier-Tinville as chief prosecutor. Because she had indeed communicated with foreign governments (her relatives were Hapsburgs) and had violated laws passed by the elected delegates of the nation she was charged with treason. During her long imprisonment she had seldom washed because she refused to display the skin of royalty to commoners. Through 18 hours of harrowing interrogation about a dozen violations, she displayed emotion only when a prosecutor suggested that she had tried to "corrupt" her son sexually. She refused to respond to the flagrant charge, and asked all mothers present to believe her. She was still clad in mourning clothes and her hair had turned to white. As her biographer, the Marquis de Segur, tells us, she was near collapse from fatigue when she returned to her cell, only to find that the verdict of guilty had already arrived.

On the morning of October 16, executioner Henri Samson came for the "Widow Capet" (a derisive reference to the dynasty that ascended the French throne in 987), bound her hands behind her back, and cut off her hair at the neck. Transported through long streets, she was the only passenger in a rustic cart, and she paid no attention to the rows of soldiers or the hostile taunting crowds that lined the way. They shouted, "l'Autrichienne, l'Autrichienne" in a rather drawn-out cadence, uttered with a tone that would make its loose translation "Austrian bitch." At noon, Samson held her severed head aloft so the multitude that thronged the Place de la Révolution could see it.

## Marat's Murderess, Charlotte Corday

Louis XVI was publicly executed in the Place de la Révolution in January of 1793, and by late spring the fury of the revolution was manifested in a contentious competition between the two more prominent political factions, the Girondins and the Jacobins. The former wished to slow the pace of the revolution, and the latter to hurry it along and eliminate any opposition. By early summer it appeared that the Jacobins, encouraged by the fiery exhortations of Jean-Paul Marat in his *Friend of the People,* were intent upon removing all Girondin influence, and possibly their heads as well.

News of these developments reached Charlotte Corday in the Norman city of Caen. She was of proud but impoverished noble stock, a descendant of the dramatist Pierre Corneille. She was well read in Roman and enlightened history, and was a firm believer in the Girondin cause as the truest form for the political direction of France—a direction that had been, in her view, wrenched from its proper course by hot-blooded Jacobins, of whom Marat was the most hideous example. She quietly arranged for a letter of intro-duction that would gain her access to meetings of the National Convention, took a stagecoach to Paris, and soon learned that Marat was not currently in attendance but at home nursing an illness. She purchased a kitchen knife with a six-inch blade, and sought an audience with Marat. After twice being turned away, she deceived his maid with a story about plots against the Jacobins in Caen, and ultimately gained entry. She stood beside his sitz bath (he suffered from scrofula and skin pustules), and then drove the knife into his chest with such force that it penetrated the aorta. Marat quickly bled to death. Corday was wrestled to the ground by a stranger as she fled the building, and turned over to the police. Her comment at that time was, "I have done my duty, let them do theirs." The word *duty* is crucial in understanding both motive and action on that July 13, a day before the anniversary of

Bastille Day. The victim was given a state funeral; his remains lie in the Pantheon.

Corday's trial was short, for she readily admitted the deed, but refused any guilt. She argued that she had merely avenged the innocent victims of the September Massacre and any others who had perished because of Marat. She said, "I killed one man to save a hundred thousand," and in a letter to a Girondin leader in Caen she frankly stated that "the end justifies the means." The theme of duty (as in Pierre Corneille's play *Le Cid*) revealed itself in her cold, detached manner as she patiently sat through the trial, arguing only on one occasion. A prosecutor inaccurately referred to the murder weapon as a stiletto, which brought immediate correction from the accused. She admonished that she was not some impassioned human of Latin blood who succumbed to fits of emotion. No, this was the calm, calculated act of a rational and honorable Norman, an act committed because of pride and obligation. Charlotte Corday was guillotined in the Place de la Révolution.

## Catherine the Great

Rumor has often distorted a quality or preference of a famous person into a believable weakness or profligacy. We have seen examples of this with Eleanor of Aquitaine and her entourage of troubadours, and of course there was a sixteenth-century Russian tsar who will forever be known to history as Ivan the Terrible. Catherine the Great (1762–1796) of Russia, at least in reputation, has probably suffered as much from such distortions as any modern European ruler of note. Indeed, according to some fabrications she was an insatiable sexual debauchee who met death when she was crushed by a rope-suspended horse with whom she was copulating. Of course, no serious scholar believes this absurd tale.

Catherine herself led the troops who secured the Russian throne for her; she was a strong, firm, and able ruler; she was an accomplished statesman, philosopher, legal codifier, and economist; and she was an enlightened correspondent of many of the century's brightest philosophers, including Diderot and Voltaire. It is true, however, that one characteristic of her administrative technique was making her successive lovers chief minister. From these chief ministers Catherine demanded and gained competent and honest service; the joys of her bed were part of the rewards of office. The French memoirist Masson, a basic source for the activities of her court, agrees that the most capable officer of Russian imperial government was the current chief minister.

Catherine presented herself at all times as a woman of substance and who warranted the respect of the untrustworthy nobility. She never engaged in vulgar or risque conversation, nor permitted it in her presence. Those who achieved both position and entry to her bed were scrutinized in a simple way, with the same methods that had been used to select adoptive emperors during the Roman Empire, when an emperor might select the best and brightest youth at court and adopt him legally as son and heir. She carefully watched men who combined political acumen with physical ability, inviting them to dine with her so that she might observe their manners, temper, and intelligence. If a man passed these first two tests, she had him thoroughly examined by the court physician. Then, and only then, did he become her personal aide, share in worldly enrichments, and join her in bed. Such men were treated much like a husband personally, and as a trusted counselor and administrator officially.

Catherine, though having embraced the Orthodox faith for obvious reasons (she was actually a German Lutheran), was quite indifferent to religious belief, so moral considerations never hindered her formula. Although the system cost her dearly financially, so did the reign of mistresses cost Charles II of England and Louis XV of France. In all, she was served by 21 lover-ministers over a 40-year period, and it is unlikely that any of them found the personal side of the relationship an onerous task. After all, one of the most famous, Grigori Potemkin, served as chief minister for eight years, and was subsequently a confidant-scrutinizer of most of those who followed him. Of Catherine he said, "When she enters an unlit room, she lights it up."

## The Great Napoleon

Most librarians would confirm that, among the holdings of their institutions, the number of volumes about or related to Napoleon

Bonaparte is exceeded only by those dealing with Jesus Christ. Thus, the great general deserves some comments.

Contrary to the portrayals by Hollywood film-makers, Napoleon did not love and lose Désirée Clary. Their families were friends, he was lonesome at military school, and his feelings for her were more on the order of a young boy's love for a good friend's older sister.

Though logic, precision, restraint, and self-discipline were hallmarks of Napoleon's conduct, in the letters he wrote to Josephine during their first prolonged separation (the Italian campaign, 1798) we find words of dripping sentimentality.

Napoleon slept but a few hours a night. He usually rose at 3:00 A.M. and had attended to all his correspondence long before his troops heard reveille. He could dictate to three scribes on three unrelated topics simultaneously, and keep all three busy without any confusion.

His marriage to Josephine was no doubt the result of his special love for her; he was a devoted husband who was never a "skirt-chaser" and did not take mistresses. However, when Polish princess Marie Walewska tossed flowers into his carriage in Warsaw, then threw herself into his bed and became pregnant, it was a most serious matter of state. It was necessary that he divorce Josephine so that a proper political marriage into one of Europe's ruling dynasties could result. In fact, the inability of Napoleon and Josephine to produce children together, though each proved able with other partners (Josephine had borne two children by her first husband), made for a most unusual case in medical history. It was even considered sufficiently important to warrant a note in the proceedings of the Royal Gynecological Society. (The fact that Josephine had reached menopause and could no longer bear children was another reason for the divorce.) The final result was the marriage to Archduchess Marie Louise of Austria and, more important, a male heir for Napoleon who, as emperor, had become royalty.

Napoleon's son, known in France as the King of Rome and in Austria as the Duke of Reichstadt, died in Vienna a short time after his father died on the island of Saint Helena. After German troops occupied Paris in June of 1940, Hitler ordered the remains of Napoleon's heir exhumed, moved to Paris, and entombed beside those of his father in the rotunda of L'Hôtel des Invalides.

Neither Hitler nor his aides ever offered any explanation for this act.

For years after Napoleon's death, and indeed well into the twentieth century, a false rumor circulated that he had died of poisoning, a belief that arose because traces of arsenic were found in his body. In truth, modest amounts of the chemical were commonly prescribed to treat syphilis, which Napoleon had contracted in Russia.

Napoleon instituted a signal corps of flagmen who sent messages in relay form from mountaintop to mountaintop. The system, which Napoleon copied from the Roman Empire, afforded the most rapid form of communication.

Except for Lucien, Napoleon appointed all of his brothers as rulers of states in his European system, and also participated in their choices of politically appropriate wives. (Lucien had already married, against his brother's instructions.) His sisters were paired with successful generals; Pauline, his favorite and the prettiest, proved to be the most troublesome. At age 17, married to General Leclerc, she was forced by her brother to join her husband on an expedition to San Domingo, in an attempt to reduce her tendency to play musical beds in Paris. The expedition's purpose was to pacify that island, a land plagued by a slave revolt led by Toussaint L'Ouverture (often called the black Napoleon because of his success at discipline). Leclerc, in 1797, succumbed to the effects of yellow fever, and widow Pauline brought his remains back to Paris with her, where she had his ears pickled and placed in an urn, which she kept on the mantel. She then wed Prince Camillo Borghese, but soon tired of him and slipped into adultery. The prince took a mistress, while Pauline returned to Paris. There she opened her lavish home to the gayest society and continued her unconcealed transgressions until, in a mirror, her brother saw her mocking his new wife and empress, Marie Louise. He banished her, with title, to northern Italy.

The Emperor's mother, Letizia, received an allowance of more than $600,000 per year, a handsome home in Paris, and many servants. She later accompanied her son during his exile at Elba, observed with sadness the climax of Waterloo, and subsequently outlived her famous son by 15 years.

Probably Napoleon's most skillful and talented minister (of foreign affairs), Prince Talleyrand proved to be one of history's most successful schemers and intriguers. He had prominently served in a similar capacity during the revolutionary govern- ments, the Directory, the Consulate, and the Empire, and ultimately served the restored Bourbons after Waterloo—one biography is entitled *The Nine Lives of Talleyrand*. Napoleon was no fool, and assessed his minister correctly. He even agreed that he could not do without his aide's superior talents. He did, however, refer to Talleyrand as "a silk stocking full of mud" (spelled *merde,* meaning animal excrement).

## *Austerlitz: The British Reaction*

In October of 1805 Napoleon and his generals so outmaneuvered 50,000 Austrian troops that the unfortunate Hapsburg command- ing officer found himself penned in on three sides with the Danube at his back. His forces were riddled by artillery, short of food and ammunition, and on the threshold of mutiny. His surrender included 30,000 prisoners. A few weeks later Napoleon so stunned the combined Austrian and Russian forces at Austerlitz that the battle has become a model for general tactics and the proper use of artillery. The French army of 73,000 suffered 8,000 casualties, while the 87,000-strong combined Russian/Austrian army saw 15,000 killed and 20,000 taken prisoner. When news of the battle reached British Prime Minister William Pitt, he offered one of the most accurate prophecies in all of history. He immediately pointed to the wall and demanded that the map of Europe there be removed, declaring, "Roll up that map, it will not be wanted in these ten years." The Battle of Waterloo occurred exactly ten years later.

# CHAPTER VI

# The Nineteenth Century

The Age of Progress is a term often applied to the period in history from the fall of Napoleon in 1815 until the opening of the Great War in 1914. Much of this designation comes from the conspicuous impact of the first industrial revolution by mid-century and the acceleration of scientific and technological processes in the four decades before the war. The period saw the strong influence of liberalism and nationalism, which contributed to wider participation in politics and education and the unification or expanded power of what we call the nation-state. The same century witnessed the long reigns of Queen Victoria (1837–1901) and Francis Joseph of Austria (1848–1916), colonial expansion, and dominance of the greater part of the world by European powers. Several scientific advances were made during this time, including the development of the theory of biological evolution, the germ theory of diseases, and the basic laws of thermodynamics. The full benefits of education, ample food, good housing, travel, and growing overall comfort were widely apparent to all serious observers as the new century arrived. But in 1914 the answer to an important historical question—whether the resources of such extensive material growth would be used for essentially peaceful purposes or, instead, employed to wage war on the largest scale imaginable—was answered.

## Questions for Discussion

- Lord Castlereagh worked harder than most to achieve a post-Napoleonic peace and European stability; possibly he even worked too hard. What personal tragedy demonstrated this?

- What British military decoration corresponds to the U.S. Congressional Medal of Honor? What is its origin?

- What word was added to the dictionaries of several nations owing to the lamentable economic and social conditions in Ireland and the resulting active resistance?

- Queen Victoria's best known prime ministers were William Gladstone and Benjamin Disraeli. How did her relations with each differ, and what might be considered the reasons for the differences?

- How did the cancan become a popular part of Parisian entertainment, and what made it so popular?

- Did Paris become a fashion center during the mid-nineteenth-century era of Napoleon III? What were some of the features of Parisian society that led many critics to label it as overdone or nouveau riche? Did the artist Daumier appreciate the latest women's fashions?

- The literary career of Victor Hugo spans the period from the 1820s to the 1880s. In what way did the preface dedication of the original version of Les Misérables reveal his devotion to humanitarian causes and how did it account for his continuing popularity in the fields of European history and literature?

- In what way did popular author Anatole France use his wit and writing skills to demonstrate what modern critics have called his desire to be accepted as a modern Voltaire?

- By what technique did the Krupp steel-producing complex of Essen impress exhibition visitors during the nineteenth century?

- Was there, historically speaking, any special timing in the inauguration of the new nation of Canada in 1867? What reason might be given for the national title "Dominion"?

- If the perfection of the automobile is to be properly viewed as a European contribution, then what features of flight give Americans special credit in its perfection?

- What facts portray the general character of Kaiser William II? As he exhibited himself to the rest of the world, might not the motto he chose for himself and his policies be termed appropriate? Did he project an image of one hostile to peace?

## The Principled Duke of Wellington

Hero of Waterloo in 1815, the "Iron Duke" remained prominent among Tory leadership in the English government, finally serving as prime minister. However, after an initial game of cards with King William IV, the duke repeatedly refused every subsequent offer to play cards with his sovereign. He simply indicated that, as a gentleman, he would not play with one who cheated, no matter who he or she was.

## The Tragic Dedication of Viscount Castlereagh

Appallingly overworked at the Congress of Vienna and by the extensive diplomatic duties of remapping Europe after Napoleon had departed from the scene, England's foreign minister was near emotional collapse by the summer of 1822. Castlereagh's most trusted comrade and closest personal friend, the Duke of Wellington, felt obligated to be honest and forthright when mental aberrations appeared: "I am bound to warn you that you cannot be in your right mind." And Castlereagh, covering his face with his hands, responded, "Since you say so, I fear it must be so." A few days later, after both pistols and razors had been removed from his quarters, he managed to get hold of a knife that had escaped the notice of his attendants, and cut his own throat.

## The "Massacre of Peterloo"

During the post-Napoleonic years (1815–1825), England experienced sporadic but frequent public disturbances in which the people demanded political solutions to economic hardships. These disturbances became sufficiently serious that on occasion the right of habeas corpus was suspended and uniformed troops were used to restore order. The most infamous episode of this period was the "Massacre of Peterloo." In August of 1819, a mass meeting of some 50,000-plus "blanketeers" (those who brought blankets to open areas where they sat and listened to radical speeches) was addressed by "orator" Henry Hunt on Saint Peter's Field in Manchester. Local magistrates, alarmed by the size of the group and the military drilling that had taken place the previous evening, ordered the arrest of the speakers. The chief constable and his officers could not break through the crowd, however, and a troop of Hussars were ordered to clear the way. Their sabres flashed, panic ensued, and in the stampede 11 people were killed and 400 injured. The "Charge of Peterloo" (alluding to the recent English victory at Waterloo) gave the government a reputation for bungling, while supplying ample material for cartoonists and pamphleteers.

At the time of this event, the poet Percy Shelley was in Italy, and upon hearing the news wrote the following lines in his *Mask of Anarchy*:

> I met Murder on the way—
> He had a mask like Castlereagh—
> Very smooth he looked, yet grim;
> Seven bloodhounds followed him;
> All were fat; and well they might
> Be in admirable plight.
> For one by one, and two by two,
> He tossed them human hearts to chew
> Which from his wide cloak he drew.

# A British Institution Is Named for Robert Peel

As Secretary for the Home Office (domestic affairs) in the Lord Liverpool Cabinet in 1823, Sir Robert Peel presided over the experimental establishment of a uniformed, but civilian, corps of police, who lived in the communities with their families, were armed with no more than a nightstick and a whistle, and answered to commissioners headquartered at Scotland Yard. By 1840 most boroughs of any significant size had copied the formula.

The "bobbies" or "Peelers" are still one of England's most cherished institutions, and popular songwriter Roger Miller has even included them in one of his songs. When founded by Peel, however, the police force received a mixed reaction, and an especially negative one from those who lived by their wits on con games in the streets of London. Some called the bobbies "raw lobsters," and others named them "blue devils." In 1833, when a bobby was killed during a riot, the jury returned a verdict of justifiable homicide. Yet in the longer tradition of history, the bobbies have come to exemplify the restraint and common sense of English life, a respected body of officers who guard the civic peace without the authoritarian show of firearms.

## The First Railway Fatality

William Huskisson had served ably in British cabinets during the 1820s alongside the reform-minded Robert Peel. He successfully lowered the tariff on grains, which in turn stabilized at a lower level the price of bread, which was so important in the diet of the lower classes. Then, in 1830, he attended the ceremonies at Rainhill for the opening of the Manchester-Liverpool Railway, where the celebrated run of Stephenson's Rocket (best prize for engine design) was featured. As Huskisson stepped out of the train to greet the Duke of Wellington, he was knocked down and fatally injured by a passing engine. The death of a cabinet minister did not make the front pages of newspapers, however, because all the front pages were devoted to the Rocket, which had performed at the staggering speed (for that time) of 36 miles an hour.

## Bavaria's Ludwig Defends His Lady

For 20 years before the revolution that racked European capitals in 1848, the modest-sized kingdom of Bavaria was ruled by Ludwig I (1825–1848), a representative of the Wittelsbach dynasty. He exhibited an aesthetic nature and tried to make Munich and Bavaria not only a center of beauty and art but also a mecca for writers and scholars. The great art galleries, opera houses, royal residences, and museums that impress tourists today date from this period. Ludwig, however, also became notorious for his amorous adventures. The most famous of these was with the Irish-born Delores Eliza Gilbert. She had swept across the European scene as the Andalusian-Moorish dancer Lola Montez, and in 1846, at age 26, managed to capture the heart of the 61-year-old Bavarian king, subsequently exercising complete sway over him until the eve of the revolution in 1848. One historian said that she aspired to become the Madame de Pompadour of the Bavarian court and nearly succeeded, while another suggested that her reputation was such that it "made you automatically think of bedrooms." Public sentiment, especially Catholic sentiment, was aroused against her, but the old king stood his ground.

When the archbishop of Munich remonstrated to Ludwig that Lola was an emissary from Satan, sent from England to destroy the Catholic faith, Ludwig responded, "You stick to your *stola* and let me stick to my Lola." Finally, resentment forced the foreign lady to seek refuge in Switzerland.

## Origin of the Victoria Cross

In 1856, the same year that saw the close of the Crimean War (Britain, France, Sardinia, and Turkey against Russia) and the Peace of Paris, the British government instituted the highest of its military decorations, the Victoria Cross. It was, and still is, open to all ranks, and so indicated a concern for the private soldier. Every Victoria Cross has been cast from the metal of melted-down Russian cannons that were seized when the British and the French captured the Crimean fortress of Sebastopol.

## The Krupp Family Steel Dynasty

The same years of the nineteenth century that saw the grand expansion of German industrial might until it rivaled that of Britain also witnessed the successful career of Alfred Krupp (1812–1887), a man of tremendous business acumen and productive energy. By the time of his death the Krupp steel works of Essen had become an international giant in basic steel fabrication and the weaponry "arsenal of the Reich." Krupp would often work in bed the whole night through, writing instructions to his agents in China, Turkey, Paris, London, and other far-off locations. He strongly believed that closeness to nature was both beneficial to health and physically inspiring. Thus he had a special bedroom constructed over the stables with the floorboards slightly spaced so that the natural odor of the manure could fill the room. In later years, his health failing, his doctors forced him to give up his favorite room.

On one occasion, in an attempt to convince German General Staff personnel of the quality of Krupp armor, he squatted behind the armor while they fired the army's best cannon at it. He stood up unscathed after the shelling, and then presented one of his new cannons, which pierced the armor. Having convinced the generals of the quality of his products, he perfected armor that could withstand the shelling of his new cannon. Although he was quite successful industrially, it was military advances that impressed Alfred Krupp the most.

Basic and fundamental contributions by his engineers, however, furnished the economic base for the future success of his steel empire. Krupp introduced and patented not only the first springs and axles of cast steel for railway cars, but also the seamless, cast-steel railway tire, in 1857, which had a great impact because it significantly reduced railway crashes caused by tires splitting at the seam of the welding. With that accomplishment the company was able to build a sound economic base for weapons experimentation. Through his daughter Bertha (after whom the large gun of World War I was named), the family went on to become armorers of Hitler's Third Reich under the direction of Alfried Krupp. Alfried was convicted of war crimes for having used slave labor during World War II and imprisoned until the early 1950s. He was freed when the West's attitudes changed during the Korean War and an attempt was made to revitalize West Germany in the wake of Cold War fears.

## Origin of the Word Boycott

Relations between British authorities and Irish rural tenant-farmers during the nineteenth century had oscillated between violence and an uneasy calm. The Irish farmers, in the 1870s, established the Land League to defend their interests; in 1880, when the House of Lords threw out a bill to compensate evicted tenant-farmers, fury blazed in Ireland. Ricks were set on fire, cattle were maimed, and men were dragged from their houses in the dark of night and assaulted (known in Irish history as "moonlighting"). Irish leader Charles Stuart Parnell suggested a new measure that came to be known as a "boycott," so named after the first person against whom it was tried. Captain Charles Cunningham Boycott had taken over a farm from an evicted tenant-farmer, and suddenly found that no one—servants, laborers, shopkeepers—would have anything to do with him. He was treated like a leper. Not only was the scheme successful, but the term found its way into many of the languages of Europe.

## Mid-Victorian England: Religion, Morals, Education

The condition of political liberty in Victorian society never ceased to astonish refugees who arrived from all parts of the Continent. Alexander Herzen, who in the 1850s emigrated from tsarist Russia, wrote, "until I came to England the appearance of a police officer in a home where I was living always produced an indefinable disagreeable feeling, and I was at once morally on my guard against an enemy. In England a policeman at your door merely adds to your sense of security." But there were also many other apparently accepted values and attitudes that were uniquely part of the Victorian scene.

Religious propriety was an understood standard. Thus, when the directors of the Counties Railway wished to run Sunday excursions from London to Cambridge, the vice-chancellor of the university hastened to point out that "such a proceeding would be as displeasing to Almighty God as it is to the Vice-Chancellor of the University of Cambridge." Volumes of some religious sermons became best-sellers. Any kind of scandal led to complete social condemnation, as Edward, Prince of Wales, discovered when he became involved in a famous divorce case in 1870. He was hissed by the crowd on the race course at Epson. It was into this society that the writings of naturalist Charles Darwin dropped with so many resounding shock waves. The Church took the offensive, and in a famous debate at Oxford Bishop Wilberforce attacked the theory as atheistic, and then asked his opponent, Thomas Huxley (who coined the term *agnostic*), whether he was descended from a monkey on his grandfather's or his grandmother's side. Huxley merely suggested that the good bishop prove Darwin wrong with the same scientific tools by which the naturalist had arrived at his conclusions.

The genuine moral fervor of Victorian society was exhibited in everything from industry to social reform, from worldwide missionary zeal to improving the nutritional content of bread. The themes in Samuel Smiles' *Self Help* exemplify this characteristic— be thrifty, virtuous, honest, hard-working, and accept rewards without being complacent. Even in relaxation many Victorians sought the strenuous life, much like that recommended later by U.S. President Theodore Roosevelt. For example, the Alpine Club was formed in 1857, and within 8 years nearly 80 peaks and passes of the Alps had been conquered by English amateurs on holiday, an achievement crowned by the climbing of the Matterhorn in 1865.

Even the educational changes and reforms of the era moved to place greater emphasis on character-building rather than on mere intellect. Organized games, not the classroom, exercised the minds of teachers and students. A cartoon in *Punch* portrayed one schoolmaster saying to a prospective pupil, "Of course you needn't work, Fitzmilksoppe, but play you must and shall."

# Queen Victoria and Her Two Great Prime Ministers

The serious student of nineteenth-century British history quickly recognizes that Queen Victoria (1837–1901) was consistently an excellent barometer for middle-class Christian ethics and values. The period of her reign from 1866 to 1886 was dominated by the careers of William E. Gladstone (Liberal) and Benjamin Disraeli (Conservative). There was a subtle friction bordering on hostility between Victoria and Gladstone, which was caused by his somewhat self-righteous demeanor, his cold and formal approach, and his failure to show sufficient deference to the queen's political role. His penchant for sprinkling his speech with biblical references and his rather condescending moral tone caused her to wish for a way to choose another Liberal leader.

With Disraeli, however, relations were always warm and cordial, a situation no doubt aided by his diplomatic sense in every corner and his keen use of careful flattery. Victoria called him "Dizzy," engaged in endearing correspondence with him, enjoyed his personal counsel, and even laid a primrose on his casket upon his death. Disraeli introduced the legislation that added Empress of India to the queen's titles. When an opportunity arose to purchase seven-sixteenths of the Suez Canal shares from the debt-ridden Khedive of Egypt, Disraeli moved swiftly. Parliament was not in session, so Disraeli requested and got an advance of 4 million pounds from the House of Rothschild. When asked what collateral he had to offer, tradition has it that the shrewd prime minister responded, "England!" He then immediately wrote to Victoria, "It is just settled; you have it Madam." This he topped off by representing Britain at the Berlin Congress of 1878, which ended a Russian-Turkish war, and returning home with a new British territory—Cyprus.

## Bismarck, the Iron Chancellor

Count Otto von Bismarck was 47 years old when he was called by William I to serve as chancellor of Prussia in 1862. Thus began an amazing career, and before it ended in 1890, Bismarck had not only resolved a constitutional crisis, but had also in his own inimitable way brought about the unification of the German states under Prussia's leadership and left his indelible stamp upon both German and world history. This dynamic statesman was quick, precise, and bombastic in both word and action, which is revealed in the following anecdotes.

His views of democracy and of the idea that political leaders would be dependent upon the whims of the masses for votes struck hard on the ears of German political figures. Bismarck said, "I am no democrat and cannot be one; I was born and raised an aristocrat." His maiden speech to the Prussian legislature included the following lines: "Not through speeches and majority decisions are the greatest questions of the day decided . . . but through iron and blood." No doubt that utterance contributed to the name by which he is best known to history—the Iron Chancellor.

He demonstrated little reservation about openly expressing his many strong hatreds. One morning he said to his steward, "I could not sleep the whole night; I hated throughout the whole night." Consistent with his general opinion of party leaders, he hated the top man of the National Liberal group, Edward Lasker. So great was the chancellor's hostility that, when Lasker died while visiting the United States and the U.S. House of Representatives sent a message of condolence to the Reichstag, Bismarck refused to transmit the message. He also hated the diminutive and vocal leader of the Catholic Center Party, Ludwig Windthorst, whom he referred to as an "evil genius." Bismarck argued that hate is as essential to a person's life as love and that both are needed for a proper balance and stability. Thus he concluded that his life was preserved and made pleasant by two things—his wife and Windthorst: "One exists for love, the other for hate."

Bismarck always considered himself a serious and active practitioner of Lutheran Christianity, and even referred to his social legislation for protection of the aged, injured, and ill as "practical Christianity." His favorite Bible verses reveal a great deal about his character. From the third Psalm, verses 7–8:

> I am not afraid of thousands of people
> That have set themselves against me round about
> Arise, O Lord; save me, O my God:
> For thou hast smitten all my enemies upon the cheek,
> Thou hast broken the teeth of the wicked.

From this one gains the impression that Bismarck believed God decided questions by the roll of iron dice and an avenging wrath.

## Louis Philippe

The July Revolution of 1830, which drove Charles X and the Bourbon dynasty from French politics, had as an outcome the elevation to the throne of Louis Philippe, of the collateral Orleanist line. Louis was the candidate of the upper-middle class, who supported him throughout his reign (1830–1848). Hence his regime took on a maintain-the-status-quo approach and resisted reform or change at every turn. That posture was best underlined by his premier during the king's last decade in power, François Guizot, who, in response to demands to lower the financial standing required to vote, said: "Enrichez-vous" (get rich).

While the "Legitimist" (Bourbon) press most often cast barbs at Louis Philippe, whose supporters rather than he himself actually represented the new wealth, probably the most memorable and popular lampoon of the "Bourgeois Monarch" was a six-part pictorial etching by the artist and friend of the working class, Daumier. Drawn in a sequence of boxes like those employed in modern comic strips, the cartoon implied that as the king's reign wore on he became fatter and began to resemble the fat cats who supported him. In the first three boxes it appears that a pear is being drawn, but by box four it is no longer certain. In box five the viewer realizes the figure is a man, and box six displays Louis Philippe in full, proper, upper-middle-class dress, but he is distinctly pear-shaped.

## The Years of Napoleon III

Prince Louis Napoleon Bonaparte was elected prince president of France in late 1848, launched a successful coup d'etat in late 1851, made himself emperor by popular plebiscite, and ruled France as benevolent dictator of the Second Empire until 1870. His mother, Hortense Beauharnais (who was Napoleon's stepdaughter), had married Louis Bonaparte (who some people say was not his father), making him the nephew of the great Napoleon. Though Louis Napoleon believed himself to be a man of destiny, the novelist Victor Hugo called him a demi-Caesar who smelled of tobacco instead of incense, and while in exile Hugo lampooned him in a novel called *Napoleon the Little*.

Until attempts upon his life demanded that he move about in secrecy, the emperor would ride in an open carriage through the streets of Paris to visit his mistress amid the cheers of citizens along the boulevards, who all knew the purpose of his journey. He was sometimes quick with a phrase, which he demonstrated after the 60-to-1 vote that made him emperor of France: "Though I have been bathed in the waters of popular sovereignty, I do not plan to live out my life with wet feet." His long administration saw the nearly complete remodeling of the streets and structures of Paris that made it the city we know today, with spacious parks, wide boulevards, and tributes to French glories in the city's monuments and streets.

## Comic Opera and the Cancan

The rage of popular Parisian theater during the 1855 exposition was musical comic opera, supported by the finances of Henry Seymour and realized in the writing-directing-producing of Johann Offenbach. No part of these productions was more popular (especially to the tourist) than the cancan, the scandal and rage of the day. The dance was discovered by French soldiers serving in Algeria, and once brought to Paris it quickly spread. Today the dance is merely suggestive, but in the era of the Second Empire the absence of underskirts made it extremely explicit. Of course, vigorous attempts to eradicate the cancan ensured not only its popularity but also its longevity.

## The Elegance and Decadence of Court-Level Society

Only the *crème de la crème* might be fortunate enough to attend a ball or reception at the Tuileries or at the great town house of a cabinet member. The conspicuous display of wealth was highly counted in this age in which material success was admired and rewarded. At a masked ball given by the new French foreign minister, Count Walewski (illegitimate son of the great Napoleon and a Polish princess), the Italian Countess Castiglione wore a Queen of Hearts costume. Corsetless, she draped her bosom in light gauze; her skirt was caught up in back, in the eighteenth-century fashion, to show the petticoat. Ornamental hearts were scattered over both bodice and skirt, invariably in interesting locations. Empress Eugénie was present that evening, but as a guest she could not command the countess to disappear before the emperor saw her. Instead, she congratulated the countess on the unique costume, but added pointedly, "Your heart seems a little low."

## Paris Becomes a Center for Tourists and Fashion

Much of the trends and practices of Louis Napoleon's Paris smacked of the characteristics that Mark Twain saw in the United States of the 1870s and 1880s. Many tourists (which were quite different from what a gentleman would term "a traveler") arrived under the auspices of an English excursion entrepreneur named Thomas Cook. By 1855 signs that read "English spoken here" could be seen in shop windows. Fashion was another concern, for it was an age of expanding prosperity characterized by all that the term *nouveau riche* brings to mind, be it negative or positive. Bright colors were definitely the *dernier cri* (last scream). French forces, allied with the Sardinians, won a great victory at Magenta in 1859, and the color magenta became the new rage in Paris. Also, brightly dyed auburn hair was considered very stylish. Although some female dress assumed masculine and military nuances, the English dressmaker Charles Frederick Worth soon rose to fame in Paris. His introduction of the crinoline (hoop skirt) was most useful to the empress, who was expecting. The style was copied by Queen Victoria, and the fashion explosion followed. The artist Daumier satirically likened the garment to a parachute.

## Napoleon III's Cousin: A Family Embarrassment

Among several members of the extended Bonaparte family whom Napoleon III saw fit to provide for politically was Prince Napoleon Jerome, the son of Napoleon's youngest brother, Jerome. During the Crimean War (1854–1856) Napoleon Jerome was made general of a division. The troops who served under him thought him a coward and hence dubbed him "Plon Plon," a name that stayed with him until his death in 1891. The term is derived from the French word *craint-plomb*, or "fear-lead." Napoleon Jerome became quite a rakish fellow, well known at the gambling and watering spas of Europe, but was again employed for political purposes when a marriage was arranged between him (aged 38) and the young daughter of Victor Emmanuel II of Sardinia.

## Problems of Authors and Artists: Flaubert, Manet, Daumier

The novel *Madame Bovary* (1856–1857) by Gustave Flaubert is still considered by most literary critics as the classic masterpiece of realism. The work was first published in serialized form in Paris, and as a result the author was prosecuted for insulting and degrading public standards of morality. The substance of the prosecution's case centered upon the two prolonged adulterous relationships of the heroine, Emma Bovary, the second of which developed because of discussions in her local cathedral. Although acquitted, Flaubert was subjected to a tongue-lashing by the judge. Here are some lines from the novel, which this writer considers to be the most erotic content in the book: "She flung off her clothes with a sort of brutal violence, tearing at her thin stay-lace so that it hissed about her feet like a slithering snake. She tiptoed across the room on her bare feet to make sure that the door was really locked, and then, with a simple gesture, let her things fall to the floor. Pale, speechless, solemn, she threw herself into his arms with a prolonged shudder." Interestingly, in the same city where this trial occurred, Paris, the cancan was being performed by dancers who wore no undergarments.

Four years later official and critical circles were shocked by Manet's unconventional painting *Olympia*. At that time, it was taboo to paint a female nude who looked real, who looked like someone you know named Fifi or like the young baker's wife at the corner shop. The nude had to be stylized in a classical sense, representing some vague ideal, as did so many Greek statues.

No artist gave more of his energy to flaying the philistinism of the bourgeoisie on the one hand and supporting the cause of the downtrodden on the other than Daumier. Artistic material also escaped the censor more readily than the printed word in journals, which had to be licensed by authorities and bonded by a large sum of caution money. One can easily visualize the following description of a Daumier lithograph: The scene is the area in front of the large display window of a pastry shop. In the foreground are two individuals who represent the bourgeois and the working class, respectively. The worker wears rustic clothing, his collar turned up against the cold, and his high cheekbones protrude from a sunken, malnourished face. The bourgeois wears shining shoes, stylish white stovepipe trousers that reveal an ample belly, a satin sash, a formal jacket with tails, and a top hat. The bourgeois stares in the shop window, where there is a lugubrious pile of cream and sugar tiers that constitutes a giant cake; the worker stares at the bourgeois.

## Victor Hugo's Compassion for the Common Man

By the late 1870s France had two conspicuous international heroes: Ferdinand de Lesseps, the builder of the great Suez Canal, and Victor Hugo. The latter had participated in every major literary genre of the nineteenth century and established a solid reputation as a liberal, humanitarian, reform-minded, patriotic son of *la belle France*. But the long trek to scholarly and artistic respect had been an arduous one. One of his many biographers, Matthew Josephson, reminds us of the lean years, when Hugo was only able to purchase a chop every third day. On the first day he ate the fat, the second he ate the lean, and on the third he sucked on the bone. Later, in his mid-70s, in letters to his closest friends he measured the status of his health not by sustained mental powers, but by the number of erections he had in a given week. There is probably no better measure of his sincerity or his temperament than the foreword dedication of the first edition of his masterpiece, *Les Misérables*. It is dedicated to the two segments of humanity that he believed are most victimized by the hypocrisy and double standards that often afflict society—women and children.

## Paris Embattled

In the Franco-Prussian War, which broke out in the summer of 1870, many French defensive positions were either methodically overrun or surrounded and forced to surrender. Napoleon III himself, along with nearly 100,000 troops, became a prisoner at

Sedan; General Bazaine and his 115,000 troops surrendered at Metz; and before Christmas Paris was encircled and intermittently rocked by Prussian artillery. As the days became weeks all supplies ran short during the particularly cold winter. Trees began to disappear from the streets and the parks when fuel supplies ran low. Only the more elegant restaurants were able to remain open, and their menus came to feature such items as elephant, zebra, and lion, while the common folk were left with dogs and rats as their only source of meat. The novelist Edmond Goncourt reported that as he walked the desolate streets, a 12-year-old girl, shivering in the darkness of a doorway, called to him and offered to go to bed with him for one piece of bread ("Monsieur, voulez-vous monter avec moi, pour un morceau du pain?").

## Anatole France: Self-Appointed Voltaire

Although less known today, and indeed given less attention by students and scholars of late nineteenth-century French literature, in his time Anatole France outsold Emile Zola, the popular author of more than two dozen novels. Anatole France did not enter the thick of the struggle between left and right, Dreyfusards and anti-Dreyfusards, or secularist and clerical, until the turn of the century. Prior to that time he prided himself on an air of cynicism speckled with either indifference to serious moral questions or the tendency to dispose of them through the use of irony (for reference see the section on Voltaire in chapter V). Some of the statements of his earlier years include the following: "Anyone who is willing to die for an idea must place a high value on conjecture"; "I have pondered the philosophy of the law, and I recognized that all social justice rests on these two axioms: theft is reprehensible, the product of theft is sacred"; and, "The law in its majestic impartiality forbids the rich as well as the poor to sleep under bridges, to steal purses and to beg for bread."

## Empress Carlota

Most accounts of the French intervention in Mexico in 1861 for the purpose of debt collection, their enlargement of troop strength,

and their eventual departure in 1866 provide plenty of information about the short career of Austrian Archduke Maximilian
(brother of Francis Joseph) as emperor of Mexico. Little is said of
his empress, Carlota, who joined him in what must have been one
of the few political marriages of the century that was also entered
into for love (Victoria and Albert excepted). Carlota married
Maximilian in 1857 at the age of 17, joined him while he served as
administrator in Milan and Venice, and accompanied him to
Mexico, where he was to be emperor (with French support), in
1864.

After the end of the American Civil War, the United States
threatened intervention against French forces; as the nationalist
supporters of Benito Juárez closed in, her husband's position
became untenable, and Carlota returned to Europe to plead for
aid in bringing him home. She gained no support from
Napoleon III, found none in Vienna, and eventually journeyed
to Rome where she pleaded with Pope Pius IX to bring pressure
on behalf of Maximilian's return. There, desolate, she refused
for a while to leave the Vatican inner chambers, fell to the floor,
and begged between sobs. In 1867 Maximilian was captured by
Juáristas and publicly executed by a firing squad. Carlota
suffered an emotional collapse from which she never recovered.
She spent her remaining years in the seclusion of castles in
Belgium and Trieste, where she lived in a state of mental
darkness until 1927.

## Ferdinand, Emperor Imbecile

With the death of Francis I in 1835, Ferdinand ascended to the
Austrian throne and created what historian A. J. P. Taylor has
called an "interregnum." The reasons were obvious, for the new
emperor (forced to abdicate in 1848) was an imbecile, epileptic,
and rickety. Some charge that his character was expressed in his
only intelligible remark: "I am the emperor and I want dump-
lings." Taylor goes on to point out what an intolerable pun this
would have been in English if the emperor had demanded pasta,
for then it would have been a noodle asking for noodles. Others
have reported at least two additional intelligible utterances by
Ferdinand. First, because ministers had to physically guide his

hand when he signed official documents, he is reported to have said, "It is easy to rule provinces; what is difficult is to write your name." Second, in 1866, long after his abdication but in front of the general staff, just after Austrian defeat at the hands of Prussian forces he is reported to have remarked, "Huh, even I could have lost those provinces."

## An Expression of Nationalism

Even for Marxists, who profess loyalty to the international working class rather than to a particular nation, it has often been difficult to repress their special identification with their own nation. At the 1879 French Worker's Congress, held in the Marseilles Folies Bergère, one delegate conceded this truth during the heat of debate, declaring that he found it difficult to embrace without reservation a doctrine "hatched by a German Jew [Marx] in a London fog."

## Anarchism as an Approach to Revolution

In late nineteenth-century France, several leftist factions, including anarchists and a variety of socialist groups, competed for public attention and the role of majority political spokesmen. The anarchists were somewhat unique in that their primary goal was simply the destruction of the existing statist structure; hence they were not tied to an elaborate ideology as the Marxists were. In criticism of his fellow leftists, one anarchist argued that during a revolution, instead of marching to the Hôtel de Ville and stupidly proclaiming a new government, "we should instead go there and shoot everyone who tries to set one up."

## The Tragedies of Emperor Francis Joseph

Despite his long reign (1848–1916), *pechvogel*, a term that means "bird of misfortune," was the name Emperor Francis Joseph chose to describe himself. No doubt the following facts about his life reveal why he called himself the bird of misfortune:

1. He married Elizabeth of the Bavarian Wittelsbach dynasty, whom he loved, and she bore him a male heir, but they drifted apart and he spent the years after 1880 as a lonely workhorse, captive of his 16-hour days at the Hofburg Palace in Vienna.

2. In 1889 his only son and heir to the Austrian throne, archduke Rudolf, joined in an apparent suicide pact with his mistress at Mayerling. Francis Joseph had the circumstances of the deaths suppressed so that his son might be buried in a proper, consecrated ceremony.

3. In 1898 Empress Elizabeth was assassinated by an Italian anarchist as she departed for a cruise on Lake Geneva. Devoid of tears, the emperor said: "I must not lament the empress. She found the death she had always desired—sudden and painless."

These personal tragedies, combined with the earlier (1867) execution of his brother Maximilian by Mexican Juáristas and the contempt he held for his only heir, nephew Francis Ferdinand (killed at Sarajevo in 1914), likely were the reasons for the emperor's self-evaluation.

Francis Joseph lived a spartan life in terms of personal habits, resisting any moves toward the use of the automobile, electric lighting, or the telephone. He lunched on sausage and pilsner, and refused to change the menu when visited by Kaiser William II of Germany. Indeed, his only pleasure away from the rigors of his office and imperial responsibilities was hunting, which he approached as a formal art. He kept a lodge at Ischl just for hunting, and refused to hunt with William II because he considered the latter a "butcher," not a true hunter.

# English Pride in an Age of Accomplishment

The third quarter of the nineteenth century presented some contradictions during a time when most informed Europeans looked with pride on a discernible and growing majority prosperity. It was also a time of visual accomplishments, some examples of which were displayed in the world expositions that became a standard part of life for major national capitals.

One sparkling example was the contribution of Joseph Paxton, a gardener-entrepreneur turned amateur architect, who was invited to a meeting in the newly constructed House of Commons and quickly observed that when a Member of Parliament addressed the assembly he could not be heard in the speaker's gallery. Positive encouragement from Lord Granville led Paxton to produce rough sketches, on a piece of blotting paper, that eventually became full plans for the famous Crystal Palace built for the London World Exposition of 1855. It was the most avant-garde spectacle that most visitors had ever seen, a gigantic, multistory structure that appeared to be a skeleton composed of cast-iron columns and girders, but had walls and a roof made of glass. Not only were the materials the most modern available, but it was also possible for the thousands of parts to be mass-produced elsewhere and then rapidly assembled on the site. This structure anticipated the twentieth century in the mid-1800s.

However, because of its huge greenhouse design and the retention of some elm trees inside, sparrows were attracted to the building, and their excrement became a rather troublesome problem. Certainly this was disastrous for the exhibitors. One sad but humorous story relates that, when asked by his queen what might be done, since firearms were ruled out by the glass, the duke of Wellington replied, "Sparrow hawks, ma'am."

## Krupp Steel Impresses the London Visitors

At the 1855 World Exposition in London, German industrialist Alfred Krupp impressed visitors with his exhibit: an ingot of his celebrated cast steel weighing 10,000 pounds and a field-gun with a steel barrel some 50 pounds lighter than the bronze ones used by the French army. (The ingot, which had been placed on the second floor of the exhibition hall, soon made its way to the first level of its own accord.) The steel magnate, who would soon be known as the "cannon king of Essen," then displayed his prowess at the use of new materials at the Paris Universal Exhibition of 1867, presenting a steel ingot weighing 80,000 pounds and, more ominously, a giant, 1,000-pound, 14-inch siege-gun. Prosperity, human inventiveness, and warfare were unfortunately intertwined during an age of optimism and growth. By the turn of the century the Krupp complex had become not only the official "armorer of the Reich," but also of half the nations from China to Turkey.

## France's de Lesseps Becomes an International Hero

Probably the technological marvel that most stirred the imagination of contemporaries and became a ready part of every schoolchild's knowledge was the successful construction of the Suez Canal, which officially opened in 1869. Ferdinand de Lesseps, who headed the great undertaking, was an entrepreneur rather than an engineer, and was already a well-known diplomat. The canal cut the distance from Europe to the East by over one-third (London to Bombay was reduced from 10,700 miles to 6,300 miles). Moreover, many technological innovations, because of the pressure of need and the concentration of talented scientists and engineers, were in close geographical interrelationship. In 1858 30,000 fellaheen laborers were working on the canal, but by the time the project was half-finished the force had been cut by three-quarters because of newly designed machinery, a fact that was quickly comprehended by British industry. A beneficial side effect was the encouragement of archaeology and Egyptology. On the negative side, none of the artists, poets, or authors of that period, nor those of the years following, were moved to commemorate the grand accomplishment or its official opening.

## War Becomes Normal

In viewing the nineteenth century as a whole (1815–1914), the third quarter stands out, not only for the triumph of machinery and a general prosperity that carried with it a better standard of living for most, but also because it was in many ways a bellicose era. The period from Waterloo (1815) until the revolutions of 1848 was one of general peace, something that also proved to be a hallmark of the era 1871–1914. Between the opening of the Crimean War in 1854 and the end of the Franco-Prussian War in early 1871, however, five wars were fought, in which every major European power was involved at least once. If the American Civil War is added (the most disastrous in loss of life), there was peace in only 6 of the 17 years.

## Garibaldi, Catalyst for Italian Unity

It was events of the period 1848–1870 that made Giuseppe Garibaldi the greatest of all Italian patriots and, by U.S. standards, the "George Washington" of modern Italy. Following the successful overthrow of papal power in Rome, Garibaldi was able to establish, with fellow nationalist Giuseppe Mazzini, a temporary "Republic," in 1849. In that same year French troops drove both nationalists from the Eternal City in a successful move for the reactionary forces. Garibaldi initially fled south, then north, east, south again, then to Tangiers, on to South America, and finally to New York City (where he made candles). He later returned to fight in the struggle to remove Austrian control from Italy. After the Austro-Sardinian War (1859) had gained for the kingdom of Sardinia-Piedmont the control of Lombardy, Garibaldi led a freebooting expedition (which was illegal according to international law) to conquer for a new nation the island of Sicily and all of southern Italy.

Garibaldi and his famous "one thousand" (and a few others), dressed in red shirts and plumed Calabrian hats, were on their way to fight a kingdom. They sailed from Genoa, with British reporters on board so that London pub debaters could digest information about the mission's progress, and landed successfully near Marsala on the west side of the island of Sicily. From there the famous "Red Man" did not stop until he had gone through the capital of Palermo, across the straits, north through Calabria, and finally to a meeting with his king in Naples. There he refused all rewards and decorations, and quietly retired to the island of Caperra, to participate again at a future date. Throughout all of this the telegraph related the progress of the "Red Man" to enthralled Europeans who gathered in pubs, salons, and clubs to hear the latest news of the expedition.

## A New American Nation Learns from the United States

Quietly and unobtrusively, in 1867 a land large enough to be called an "empire" became an independent state known as the Dominion of Canada. In ceremonies presided over by an indomitable John A. Macdonald a new nation was born on the northern border of the United States, a nation that demonstrated clearly by its constitution that it had learned from the fratricidal war that had ripped apart the republic to the south. Contrary to the formula of the U.S. Constitution, that of Canada reserved to the federal government "all powers not specifically delegated to the states."

The difficulty Canadian leaders experienced in selecting an appropriate name for the new nation may be of special interest to students of the extensive scope of history. The group of God-fearing, Christian gentlemen, most of whom were of Scottish or English Protestant heritage, were in search of a name for a responsibly governed nation that stretched from the Atlantic west to the Pacific and north to the Arctic. It was the Christian element that proved crucial because, for the Christian, *empire* is an unhappy term, as it was an empire that crucified Jesus and persecuted his loyal followers and the term was always used in connection with evil in the Bible. The term *dominion*, however, is lavishly used in Scripture to express God's power and the powers he granted to humans. So, in 1867, the Dominion of Canada joined the states of the world as a prime player in the British Empire.

## Ethnic Animosity in the Austrian Empire

There were many pockets of anti-Semitism that disturbed the European scene in the late nineteenth century, but the conspicuously polyglot character of the Austrian Empire afforded many levels and degrees for the exhibition of racial and ethnic prejudice. In fact, there was no clear majority of any kind except in select regions. The Austrian Empire included Germans, Italians, Slovenes, Czechs, Slovaks, Serbs, Croats, Magyars (Hungarians), Ruthenians, Poles, and, of course, Jews.

It was into this very world, whose capital of Vienna was an ethnic melting pot, that Adolf Hitler was born and reared before World War I. The Jews from the east (*Ost Juden*) were set apart by their peculiar clothing, beards, and customs, traits that often irritated Westernized and assimilated Jews such as the Rothschild banking family of Vienna. The German nationalist Heinrich von Treitschke noted "that year after year there pours in from the inexhaustible Polish reservoir a host of ambitious pants-selling youngsters, whose children and children's children will someday control . . . the stock exchanges and newspapers." In his writings (or ravings), one Father Sebastian Brunner repeatedly called the Jews swine, and one Austrian politician posted above the gate of his estate the statement, "Dogs and Jews must not enter."

In the Magyar (Hungarian) half of the empire, there was harassment of all "lesser" peoples who were not of Magyar ancestry and language. For example, despite an increase in the Slovak population, between 1869 and 1911 the number of basic schools employing the Slovak tongue decreased from nearly 2,000 to only 440. Two common Magyar sayings were, "When a Slav speaks a dog yelps," and, "A dog will never become bacon." Despite protests at home and from intellectuals throughout Europe, the process called Magyarization was continued in brutal fashion until the outbreak of World War I.

## Proving the Impact of Technology

Between 1850 and 1913 more than 70 percent of the world's manufacturing was centered in just four countries—Germany, Great Britain, France, and the United States. Viewing the trends around him at the turn of the century, German economist Werner Sombart (1863–1941) pointed out some startling facts in his *German National Economy in the Nineteenth Century*. Not only had humans harnessed nature with machines that duplicated human capacities, but they had also gone on to create, through the forces of technology, machinery to perform what no quantity of humans could do. Nothing rendered this more clearly than the simple examination of what we call horsepower. Germany in 1907 possessed 4,345,047 horses. Yet the locomotives alone in Germany represented more than 12 million horsepower. To replace the contemporary machine-produced horsepower with horses would have left no room on earth for people or trees. Technology and machinery were responsible for the great productivity that caused historian David Thomson to declare that within a single lifetime European families became healthier and better fed, cleaner and better housed, more literate and better informed, and enjoyed the highest standard of living in the world.

However, it was also clear that if these productive forces were concentrated for the purpose of warfare, humankind would witness the worst and biggest war known to history, which it did from 1914 to 1918. Progress indeed has its drawbacks.

## Goodbye to Gaslight

In 1867 German industrialist Werner Siemens proudly announced that "technical science now has the means of generating electric current of unlimited strength, cheaply and conveniently, at any place where driving power is available." Generators driven by steam engines had for some time limited the size of an area that could be served with electricity. A marvelous example of this new capability occurred on August 25, 1891. The mayor of Frankfurt-am-Main opened an electro-technical exhibition by throwing a single switch, which bathed the entire exhibit district in the light from a thousand lamps and set hundreds of motors and machines humming. Proudly he announced that the current had been brought to Frankfurt over a distance of 110 miles from a hydroelectric plant on the Neckar River. This was the first long-distance, high-tension transmission line (15,000 volts), built under the direction of the brilliant young Munich engineer Oskar von Miller.

## Revolutions in Transportation

Largely due to the pioneering work of Gottlieb Daimler with multiple-cylinder motors and gasoline carburetors, and improvements on Daimler's work by Carl Benz during the period 1885–1900, the automobile is usually considered a European invention. The airplane, on the other hand, was the first spectacular technological breakthrough of the United States. Even though the French had worked for years (Bleriot and Levavasseur) to develop powered flight, they had failed, largely because they attempted to design aircraft that operated in much the same manner as autos. Thus they resorted to progressively more powerful engines, which in each case weighed more and defeated the purpose. The Wright brothers' work was instead premised upon observations of birds and their use of air currents. As a result the Wrights built gliders that functioned much like birds, with the aim of keeping weight at a minimum and making the best possible use of natural air movements. The most crucial problem of early flight was thus solved.

## *The Dangerous Kaiser William II*

Observations by associates combined with his own statements provide for us a rather disturbing picture of Kaiser William II, who led Germany into the disaster we know as World War I. A sampling follows.

"Everyday is a masquerade ball for the monarch," commented one observer, noting that the bombastic kaiser had ordered no less than 37 changes in uniform style for the imperial guard in a span of 16 years.

William II's first public proclamation upon becoming kaiser was not to his people but to "my army." Everyone close to him knew that he was happiest when visiting the barracks. To new recruits he once said, "When your emperor commands you to do so you must shoot at your fathers and mothers." When addressing the contingent of German marines about to depart to help quash the nationalist Boxer Rebellion by the Chinese, he advised the soldiers to "act like Huns." Thus it did not require much propagandist innovation to apply that term to the German troops during World War I.

When the kaiser, a lover of travel, visited Palestine he appeared at holy shrines in the uniform of a medieval crusader, cross and all. At a naval review during the opening of the Kiel Canal he stood at attention, saluting, wearing the costume of the mythical "Flying Dutchman." Only the strongest restraint applied by his aides during a trip to Rome prevented him from appearing at the Museum of Antiquities in the full regalia of an ancient Roman general.

He commonly referred to leaders of the several political parties represented in the Reichstag as either "nightwatchmen" or simply "sheepsheads." The kaiser declared that if the leader of the Catholic Center Party ever visited his palace he would merely have the man collared by three guards "and thrown out."

His reply to the manifesto that announced the world's first international peace conference, to be held at the Hague, was as follows: "Can we picture a supreme warlord abandoning his historic regiments . . . and thus delivering his cities over as prey to anarchists and democrats?" He apparently saw little difference between the two groups. Then he added, "I trust in God and my unsheathed sword, [then quietly to an aide] and I shit on all resolutions of international conferences." Maybe this attitude partly accounts for the comment that his head teacher at Kassel added to William's report card when he completed *Gymnasium:* "Conceit is no substitute for hard work."

It is probably true that the able Chancellor Bismarck saw what was coming when, in 1890, William asked for his resignation. The kaiser addressed the departure of his minister this way: "The duty of watchkeeping officer in the Ship of State has now devolved upon me; the course remains the same, full steam ahead."

# CHAPTER VII

# The Twentieth Century

The selections for this chapter have been chosen to provide interesting sidelights or introductions to developments, events, and personalities of the period 1900–1945. The first few anecdotes are confined to the years that led to World War I, followed by revealing tales of the various kinds of impact the war had on troops at the front and civilians at home, and then by stories about the interwar period. There was disillusionment with the prospects for peace following the World War I, and many faced economic hardships that, when combined with the devastation caused by the Great Depression, by 1931 led to despair. During this period there was a fear of spreading Bolshevik revolution, and Western leaders witnessed the collapse of democratic governments accompanied by the victory of authoritarian or fascist interests. Ultimately, the democracies faced the reality of general aggression and the prospect of a second war even more terrible than the Great War. Both developments contributed to a vast transformation of life for citizens on both sides of the Atlantic and in Asia as well. The impact of rapid change, fostered by pressing needs of war and a phenomenal increase in power, would be felt in nearly all aspects of life. This change would be so fundamental that such fields as medicine, transportation, food processing, chemistry, housing construction, and forms of entertainment were conspicuously altered. Additionally, as all statesmen after 1945 became startlingly aware, the backdrop of life on this planet was now shadowed by a possible nemesis—the ultimate bomb.

## Questions for Discussion

- What interesting custom did former President Theodore Roosevelt observe while dining with dignitaries of the Austro-Hungarian Empire?

- By what methods or actions did Joseph Stalin make special contributions to the Bolshevik Party during the prewar era?

- What did Lenin offer as qualifications to be a good leader in the cause of revolution? How did he propose to handle the millions of Russians who might disagree with or resist his plans?

- Was France's desire to regain the provinces of Alsace-Lorraine a contributing factor to war in 1914?

- Who was Lord Grey? Why do you think he spoke of the "lamps" going out in the world? Was he right?

- In hindsight, taking into consideration the span of European history since the eleventh century (William the Conqueror), just how big a war was World War I?

- What rather unique technique was employed in various German towns by 1916 as a means to raise funds for the war effort?

- What does the cost in human lives tell us about twentieth-century warfare?

- What were some of the collateral developments arising from wartime conditions—expanded role of government, social life in the pub, more earnings, conscription or resistance to it, rationing, censorship, transportation—that came to have an impact on civilians at home? Why was Lord Rhondda nicknamed the "jam king"?

- Did Clemenceau believe that peace entailed more than the mere absence of war?

- What secretive Sicilian organization has come to have a profound influence in both U.S. and Italian history? Did such influence invade politics and elections? What is the origin of the word *mafia*?

- Supply an example of Hitler's conduct that might support the contention that even in his earlier years he was a man easily remembered by those who had contact with him.

- In light of interwar history, what, if any, advice might a teacher offer to students before they viewed the award-winning film *Cabaret*?

- What example of the French lack of preparedness has been supplied by the writer André Maurois?

- What unusual technique for intimidating opposition leaders was used by Italian fascists, and how might it conceal the more visible result of terrorist practices?

- What might a teacher relate to youth today to enhance their understanding of World War II in terms of size, production, shortages at home or abroad, electronic deception, transportation, the Allies, and the motivation to employ the atomic bomb in the Pacific theater of the war?

## Irony of the World Peace Movement

Aided by the inspired leadership of the devoted and energetic Baroness von Suttner and philanthropists from many different nations, the world peace movement of the late nineteenth and early twentieth centuries culminated in two grand conferences held at the Hague in the Netherlands, first in 1899 and again in 1907. Never in history had so many prominent personalities and so much economic support been concentrated in an international move to prevent war and reduce armaments. Yet, the historical record shows that during the very decade enclosed by the two meetings the size of armies and production of armaments increased anywhere from 25 to 50 percent, the latter increase being that of Russia, whose Tsar Nicholas II (1894–1917) served as the grand convener of the 1899 meeting. In most nations such figures did not include naval construction, in which there was a race between Britain and Germany. Figures for the remaining years leading to the summer of 1914 show even greater increases.

## Table Manners at an Imperial Dinner

Theodore Roosevelt has reported how impressed he was with his travels to European capitals as a former U.S. president. He did, however, express modest revulsion at a custom he observed while attending a state dinner at the beautiful and spacious Schönbrunn Palace of Emperor Francis Joseph in Vienna. Curious about medium-sized bowls of water that were next to the plate of each guest, Roosevelt waited to see how others might use them, assuming that they were probably finger bowls. Much to his surprise, the guests used the water to flush their mouths in the style of a mouthwash, then spit the fluid back into the same bowl and reused it after the next course. The bowls remained on the table throughout the meal.

## Stolypin's Neckties
## Fight Terror and Murder

By the time Peter Stolypin became prime minister to Tsar Nicholas II (1894–1917) and the first Duma had met and dissolved, Russian civil disorder threatened to destroy any prospect of successful reform. Stolypin was probably the most able Russian minister in modern imperial history, but along with well-planned agrarian and educational reforms there was a need to pacify the nation, for terror was everywhere. During 1906 and 1907 alone 4,000 officials were murdered and major bank robberies numbered in the dozens. Hence the government resorted to the tactic of traveling judicial officials who accompanied police in their searches for wanted criminals. When apprehended, the violators could be tried immediately and, if convicted, executed by hanging from the closest strong tree limb. Because of the necessary frequency of this practice, the tools of the execution came to be known as "Stolypin's neckties."

## The Early Career of Joseph Stalin

The Congress of Russian Social Democrats (Menshevik and Bolshevik), held at Stockholm in 1907, authorized Lenin to organize a quasi-underground Military Technical Bureau to defend loyal operatives within Russia from extralegal attacks by rightist thugs. Under this cover Lenin sanctioned a small clique to carry out "expropriation" raids and make them appear to be the work of free-lance desperadoes beyond party control. The appearance that "outsiders" had perpetrated the raids would alleviate the requirement to reveal the spoils to the party as a whole, and therefore the benefits could be fed directly to the

Bolshevik faction. Squads of this type perpetrated some daring robberies in Moscow, in St. Petersburg, and in many important provincial cities.

In the Caucasus region operations were directed by a sullen, pock-marked Georgian, a former theological student named Josef Vissarionovich Dzhugaskvili, who used the conspiratorial pseudonym Koba and the pen-name Stalin (which means steel). He was both a director and frequent participant, and his field commander was a tough, cross-eyed, incredibly daring Georgian named Tev Petrossian, alias Kamo, a kind of Jesse James of the Bolshevik wing of the revolutionary movement. How well the retinue of highwaymen-comrades knew Marxist principles is not known, but they were experts at ambushes and bomb-making. The Stalin-Kamo team was responsible for a series of train and bank robberies, fought with police-like guerrillas, and aided escapes by captured comrades. Stalin personally supervised the famous Tiflis stagecoach robbery in the summer of 1907, which netted $100,000 in Russian banknotes. The Bolshevik ambush employed bombs and grenades thrown from rooftops, destroyed a contingent of Cossack guards, and escaped with the funds to Berlin. And all along millions of people thought Lenin meant legal confiscation of some type when he repeatedly used the term *expropriation.*

## *A German General Scoffs at Peace*

In 1911, during the period between the second Hague conference on international peace and the explosion of August 1914, General Friedrich von Bernhardi published a book entitled *Germany and the Next War,* a study in military analysis and prophecy. By 1913 the work had reached its sixth edition and was widely spreading vulgarized misrepresentations of the philosophies associated with Nietzsche. On one hand war was seen as a natural expression of the German mood, and on the other hand as an example of the Darwinian concept of survival of the fittest as applied to the modern state system of the twentieth century. Bernhardi was an influential military author and hence his views carried great weight with the appropriate elites at home and abroad. The prominent general asserted that the desire for peace is not only hopeless and utopian but "immoral and inhuman." War, said Bernhardi, "is not only a necessary element in the life of people, but also an indispensable factor in culture, indeed the highest expression of the strength and life of truly cultured peoples."

He openly advocated a final reckoning with France, insisting that for the Germans there was only one alternative, "World Power or destruction." Strong, sound, and flourishing peoples, declared Bernhardi, increase in population and need constant expansion of their frontiers to accommodate such growth. Since the earth was already so fully colonized, land had to be won at the expense of others, by conquest. War and conquest, therefore, are necessities.

## Colonel Alfred Redl, Prewar Spy

In May of 1913 the Viennese press revealed that Colonel Alfred Redl, then serving as chief of staff of the 8th Army Corps in Prague, had committed suicide. Authorities revealed few details, merely indicating that he had been selling secret military information to a foreign power (Russia). The fascinating events of his career were never revealed completely, until Austrian archives were examined by occupation experts and journalists following World War II. At that time all the sinister demimonde activities of his special world and his rise to the position of chief of Austro-Hungarian counter-espionage activities by 1900 came to light. While the affair offered all the juicy aspects of a spy-thriller, some observations about Redl and his fate are of particular interest to the historian:

1.  Except for the fondlings of his adolescent years at military school, Redl's first unrestrained sexual experience was with a young female circus performer, a single occasion from which he contracted syphilis. This condemned him for the rest of his life to regular doses of silver nitrate, the chief pre-penicillin treatment used to arrest the disease and prevent its development to a second or third stage. From that point forward he was a practicing homosexual, as was the Russian nobleman who originally debauched him and snared him into selling national secrets. The

blackmail came after his deeper involvement in the traffic of information and the elevated importance of his military rank.

2. He was never rewarded lavishly by the Russians, but rather was usually pressed for funds in order to support a handsome but flighty spendthrift lieutenant, whom he passed off as his nephew.

3. After his investigators and accusers had confronted him with the evidence of his obvious treason, his brother officers furnished him with a revolver. The delegation then paced the carpet outside his bedroom awaiting the sound of the penitential shot.

4. The use of ritual suicide for the sake of military honor destroyed the relationship between the heir to the throne, Archduke Francis Ferdinand, and army Chief of Staff Conrad von Hoetzendorf, for two very serious reasons. First, the archduke was a devout Catholic, and this situation had made the Catholic monarchy an accomplice to suicide. He was shocked. Second, on the practical side, the archduke was furious that the officers had forced Redl to blow his brains out before he had revealed everything he knew about Russian espionage operations.

# Lenin Speaks on Leadership and Population Removal

According to historian David Shub, Bolshevik leader Vladimir Lenin had a simple formula for the proper way to supervise an unfolding revolution: "A central committee, to be effective, must be made up of gifted writers, able organizers, and a few intelligent scoundrels." While visiting the University of California at Berkeley the late, eminent twentieth-century British mathematician and philosopher Bertrand Russell recounted how he had once conversed with the Communist leader during one of Lenin's visits to London prior to World War I. Russell asked how Lenin planned to deal with the more than ten million prosperous and wealthy farmers in Russia should the Bolshevik revolutionaries succeed in overthrowing the existing regime. Lenin paused before answering. A spark seemed to flame from his eyes at the same time that a pleasant look overtook his face, and then he said calmly and joyously, "We'll kill them."

## Rasputin: Mad Monk or Political Genius?

The surviving photographs of Grigory Yefimovich Rasputin portray either his true self or the image he wished to exhibit as part of his shrewd game in his rise to influence at the highest center of power in Russian imperial government. The photographs show a sturdy man of medium height dressed in a peasant blouse, loose trousers, and large boots. He had a large, fleshy nose, long, brown, poorly combed hair that was parted in the middle, and a wiry, unkempt beard that was long and dark. He had deep-set eyes that were supposedly steel blue, with pupils that shrunk to pinpoint size when he concentrated. Here was a genuinely sinister scoundrel who did his best to look like one. From the information we have he was a hoax, grafter, drunkard, blasphemer, debauchee, and trickster. In his early years he was a town brawler with the grossest of manners, someone who dipped his hands in the fish soup when he ate and seldom, if ever, bathed. He played the role of the "great unwashed" right down to scratching his behind in public. Some additional facts will help to explain his rise to paramount influence.

Well before his arrival in St. Petersburg Rasputin established the reputation of a wandering rural revivalist and soothsayer-healer. He won this role as a kind of holy man and lay religious teacher by his extensive travels and worship, in the Near East and throughout Russia, before the best-known sacred shrines. His gifts as a healer, though doubtless mainly dependent on mental suggestion, proved his skills were not bogus. Rather than a monk, he was a self-anointed *strannik,* a holy man who was saved and afforded gifts from God owing to his having repented after sin, hence reaching the humblest position one can achieve. According to this doctrine it is almost better to have sinned, become the most knowledgeable of sin, and then repented than never to have sinned at all. His filth, stinking rags, and mournful eyes merely attested to the genuineness of his repentance. We are reminded of how North African Muslim leaders allowed no harm to come to Saint Francis during his pilgrimage there because, as one of them said, his unkempt personage was the true mark of a Christian holy man.

Rasputin's entry into influential circles of the imperial court in St. Petersburg came when he demonstrated his healing talents by successfully treating a favorite hunting dog of Grand Duke Nicholas after the animal had been given up for dead. Hence he quickly came to the attention of Grand Duchess Militsa, a woman devoted to seers, mediums, and various quasi-ecclesiastical mystics. This accomplishment was followed by some accurate predictions of future events, especially that Tsarina Alexandra would finally deliver a male child. Two factors aided his influence with Alexandra: her decidedly hysterically religious character, tempered by a strongly superstitious nature, and the dangerous hemophilia that afflicted the tsarevitch, Alexis, the only direct male heir to the imperial throne. Both Nicholas II and Alexandra, obsessed with the health of their child, were extremely vulnerable to quackery in pious clothing.

Despite the efforts of some members of the court circle, Rasputin confirmed once and for all the tsarina's confidence in his healing powers when, in 1912, Alexis, who was near death from internal hemorrhages, rallied to recovery after receipt of a telegram from the strannik, who was in far-off Siberia. Though Rasputin employed Tibetan remedies and had taken instruction in professional hypnotism, Alexandra believed that his extraordinary tranquilizing powers were solely of spiritual origin and that he was capable of the kind of miracles that only saints could perform.

By 1909 and thereafter Alexandra's correspondence to both Rasputin ("I kiss your hands . . . lean my head on your beloved shoulders") and her husband ("only believe more in Our Friend") reveal clearly the nearly pathological dependency that characterized her attitude toward the holy man. Even when informed by trusted relatives that Rasputin had been seen in embraces with several different married women of the court, Alexandra simply responded that the Apostles had also embraced.

While the intricacies of Rasputin's influence or his villainy and boorishness need little further comment, the circumstances of his death are most interesting, especially since many of the specific details were revealed in a New York courtroom more than a half century after the event.

The central actor in the Rasputin murder was none other than the tsar's nephew, Prince Felix Youssoupoff. He was present in the New York courtroom with hopes that his testimony would be worth $1.5 million, the amount for which he had sued the Columbia Broadcasting System for damages resulting from their 1963 television dramatization of the murder. The prince said he persuaded Rasputin to come to the family's Moika palace, where he and three other conspirators had poisoned wine, tea, and cakes waiting. Youssoupoff said he sang to the monk as he ate, expecting him to die quietly, but Rasputin only became mildly sick and acted drunk, asking the prince to sing some more. Upstairs the sound from a gramophone playing "I'm a Yankee Doodle Dandy" could be heard, and the prince said they would all go upstairs after some guests had departed. According to the prince, the three conspirators were amazed that Rasputin was not dead, and Grand Duke Dmitri gave Youssoupoff his gun, saying, "We must kill him." The prince said he approached Rasputin as he sat in a chair, told the monk to pray, and then shot him at close range in the heart and liver. Rasputin still had the strength to leap at his host and try to throttle him. Then the victim ran out into the palace courtyard and fell in the snow. A second conspirator took the gun from the prince and fired three more shots into the victim, but still he did not die. "I then took a truncheon and beat him over the head and tried to kill him," Youssoupoff testified. Finally, the monk appeared lifeless, and Grand Duke Dmitri threw the body in the nearly frozen Neva River in back of the palace. The prince said he was placed under house arrest for about a month, then allowed to go south to the Crimea with his wife. When asked about motive, Youssoupoff said that Rasputin claimed to be a German agent and that he had to stay at the imperial court. The prince insisted, however, that the real motivating factor was the false monk's loathsome sexual debaucheries.

## Alsace-Lorraine: A Cause of War?

In the spring of 1967 this author was fortunate enough to join other colleagues in a small luncheon with senior French statesman and the former premier of the Fourth French Republic Pierre Mèndes-France. Thus I was able to ask Mèndes-France whether revenge for, and the return of, Alsace and Lorraine was a significant motivating factor for France to go to war in 1914. After all, more than two generations had passed since the loss of the province in 1870 and certainly only a small fraction of the French population could personally remember the occasion of the loss (i.e., Clemenceau). Our guest's answer was less than direct, but made his view crystal clear. Reminding us that he was in elementary school in the pre–World War I years, he went on to point out that all school classrooms had at the front a large map of western Europe. France was one color, Germany another, and the "sister provinces" were conspicuously represented in violet, the French color of mourning. Young students were reminded of the loss of Alsace-Lorraine no less than six days a week.

## The Very Last Step to World War I

In response to Russia's commencement of general mobilization, the German government issued, on July 31, an ultimatum to the Russian government, demanding that mobilization cease within 24 hours or a state of war would exist between the two empires. What follows is a description of what occurred the next day in the offices of the Russian Foreign Minister Sazanov, which reveals the details of the toughest of all diplomatic jobs in Europe on August 1, 1914.

At 7:00 P.M. on August 1, Count Friedrich von Pourtalès, the German ambassador to Russia, his face revealing the effects of a week of strain and lack of adequate sleep, entered the office of Sazanov, a congenial man who was no doubt agitated at the time. Formally, and rather hurriedly, the German asked whether the Russian government had chosen to respond affirmatively to the ultimatum, as the stated deadline had passed some seven hours before. Not receiving a clear or precise answer, the German repeated the question. The Foreign Minister repeated what he had said many times before—the Russians could not issue any order to demobilize, but were willing to continue with negotiations for a peaceful resolution of differences between their two nations. The count paused, then reached into the side pocket of his coat and removed a piece of paper that he had carried since the day before. He never wished, and in fact was repelled by the possibility, that it would be delivered. He unfolded it, then read out loud, and breathed harder with each sentence as he approached the final statement: "His Majesty the Emperor, my august sovereign, accepts the challenge in the name of the Empire and considers himself at war with Russia."

All of this took place between two men who were old friends, of the same class and the same world, men who had enjoyed the ballet or a fine cigar together. Pourtalès began to lose control of himself as he slowly realized that he was about to lose an entire way of life. He ran to the window, looked out at the heights of the Winter Palace in the evening sun, and broke into tears. Sazonov placed a hand on his shoulder. The two diplomats embraced in Russian fashion, but for the last time.

## Lord Grey, British Foreign Minister

Just two days after Count Pourtalès suffered the obligation of presenting a declaration of war to an old friend, British Foreign Secretary Lord Grey stood with bowed shoulders at the window of the Foreign Office. He too seemed to see the same tragedy envisaged by the German ambassador: the loss of a way of life and a particular world in which all had felt comfortable. With apparent full comprehension of the irreparable damage that the war would inflict on the social order he knew and loved, he uttered the words that would furnish the future title of a book on World War I and that tragically portrayed the sentiment of the chilling vision: "The lamps are going out all over Europe; we shall not see them lit again in our time."

The statement is an interesting comparison to William Pitt's remark to "roll up the maps" upon receiving news of Napoleon's crushing victory over Austria and Russia at Austerlitz. It is probably of even greater historical meaning to note that top British political leaders in the 1920s, 1930s, and during World War II were members of the same age group that had led Britain during World War I. The drain of human beings caused by the 1914–1918 era rendered the spontaneous judgment of Lord Grey an ominous and accurate prophecy.

## Calmette, Le Figaro, and Murder

During the fortnight that followed the assassination of Archduke Francis Ferdinand at Sarajevo, readers of the dozen-plus Parisian dailies were treated to the unfolding intricacies of a juicy scandal that involved personages of high public profile and issues of patriotism and personal morality. Finance Minister M. Caillaux, a spokesman for economic cooperation with Germany who was fiercely opposed to the three-year law to expand French military forces, was locked in a heated mass-media struggle with the ultrapatriotic publisher of the bellicose daily *Le Figaro*. The culmination came when the second and current Madame Caillaux was threatened by the publisher with revelation of her private love letters for the purpose of bringing political pressure on her husband. The letters had been written when she was both the minister's mistress and the wife of another. The letters had been stolen by the first Madame Caillaux and passed to publisher Gaston Calmette, who threatened to publish them. The second Madame Caillaux simply went to the newspaper offices and shot Calmette to death. For her crime of passion a jury acquitted Madame Caillaux. All this was going on in Paris while Austrian leaders prepared an impossible ultimatum for Serbia that would trigger a world war.

## *The Historical Scope of World War I*

In sixteenth-century Europe (the age of religious wars and the Spanish Armada) war killed or wounded perhaps 1 combatant in 20. In the eighteenth century (Frederick the Great, Catherine the Great, American and French Revolutions, Napoleon) the ratio was about 1 in 7. As of 1925, the ratio had become 1 in 3. Understanding that the Allied and Associated Powers called more than 42 million men to serve and the Central Powers (Germany, Austria, Hungary, Bulgaria, and Turkey) called over 22 million, we arrive at a combined figure of nearly 28 million men dead or wounded. This simple arithmetic reveals that between 1900 and 1925 more men died or were wounded on European battlefields than in all of the preceding eight centuries. The figures are so startling that they have led sociologist Pitirim Sorokin to observe a direct correlation between the advance of civilization and the deadliness of war.

# Managed News about the Progress of the Great War

Nations on both sides of a war that dragged on with a tremendous cost of human life and materials sought to convince their own citizens as well as the rest of the world of the rectitude of their cause. Hence well-managed propaganda, sometimes even concocted, furnished news reports became an integral part of the war effort. So much did this become true that a British M.P. asserted that if all the victories he had heard reported were true, then western forces by 1918 should have been in Vladivostok.

## The British Fabricate War Stories

General J. B. Charteris (in the *New York Times*, October 20, 1925) recounted how the caption under a picture showing trains loaded with horse carcasses was switched with another that depicted German war dead. The picture and underlying explanation was then released to the Chinese press so that the populous nation with a traditional reverence for the dead would believe Germans used the remains of humans to produce fertilizers and munitions. The general, who had served as head of British Army Intelligence, was astonished at the worldwide circulation the erroneous story received.

## Fabricated Atrocity Stories

Through fabrication and similar methods many so-called stories of atrocities were released purporting to expose German misconduct in an attempt to influence neutral nations. To influence Catholics, there was a story of the hanging of two priests in Belgium, each suspended from ropes on the arms of a large cathedral bell. Being of precisely identical weight, their bodies seemed to keep the ringing in perpetual motion. There were pictures of babies being tossed in the air and impaled on German bayonets, and of the kaiser, in a ceremonial helmet with a spike on top of it, who chopped off the hands of little children as they passed by his block and ax. To appeal to Americans who lived far inland and thus could not identify with the U-boat threat as a Bostonian could, there was the story of how the kaiser wished to take over the world and might have his castle located in some central spot like Kansas.

## Rumors Circulate through the Front Lines

There were, as well, many rumors that circulated widely in battlefield areas, but that also reached the press in distant locations. One of these claimed that the Germans crucified a Canadian soldier in the midst of the no man's land that separated armies, where he could not be saved but could be observed through field glasses; Paul Fussel (*The Great War in Modern Memory*) notes that this story reached the readers of the *Los Angeles Times.* Another rumor, which was printed in the *British Evening News,* related how English bowmen who had fallen at Agincourt (1415) appeared to thwart German operations during the retreat of British forces at Mons. Professor Fussel claims that the masterpiece of all wartime rumors described the operations of a battalion-sized group of half-crazed deserters from all armies that existed between battle lines. They lived underground in abandoned trenches and dugouts or caves, "living in amity and emerging at night to pillage corpses and gather food and drink." Evidence indicates that the rumor was commonly accepted by many of the troops, even leading to the belief that the hordes grew to such number that gas was used to exterminate them at war's end.

## An Inventive Technique
## To Raise War Funds

One of the more unusual techniques for raising funds to support the war effort belonged to Germany. During the conflict all larger German cities put up wooden statues of Commander in Chief Hindenburg, into which those who made a contribution were permitted to drive an iron nail. Professor Walter Goerlitz (*German General Staff*) considered the idea a vulgarism, but much of what humans have been forced to resort to in modern war fosters the vulgar. It certainly was not as romantic as cinema idols Douglas Fairbanks, Sr., and Mary Pickford hawking war bonds in Times Square.

## British Advice for Parents of U.S. Troops

The official view of Lord Northcliffe, publisher of the *London Times*, was that a soldier should look upon his duty as a fortunate development, something that might bring envy from those stuck with the drab routine of life on the home front. When the Yanks entered the fray, he suggested to uninformed Americans what they might send their soldier boys at the front—peppermint bull's-eyes (candy). He indicated that they warmed soldiers when sucked during the chill of night, and though they also provided digestive benefits, this was not crucial, since at the front digestion was never a problem. All of the fresh air, generous feeding, regular exercise, and freedom from domestic worries or responsibilities kept the front-line soldier in superb health and humor. This account must be placed next to the words of Leonard Thompson (in Ronald Blythe's *Akemfield*), who served at Gallipoli: "We were all so lousy and we could not stop shitting because we had caught dysentery. We wept, not because we were frightened, but because we were so dirty."

## The High Cost of an Offensive on the Western Front

In June of 1916 General Douglas Haig launched a British offensive in the region of the Somme that remains one of the greatest disasters in military annals. On the first day alone, the British suffered 60,000 casualties out of the first 110,000 to attack. When the entire operation finally ground to a halt before solid German defenses, the British and Germans had suffered casualties at a rate of 420,000 and 445,000, respectively. The British had managed to claim seven miles of pock-marked soil on a seven-mile front.

## Conditions of War Expand the Use of Obscenities

Partly as a result of vulgar and obscene songs concocted by the English Tommies in the trenches, which they possibly did to relieve the monotony and dreariness of life on the front, the worst four-letter word became a common part of the English language. At least, it was the wartime era and experience that brought recognition of the word in literature. At that time, however, it usually appeared as some fabricated variation such as "mucking" or "flicking" (like the present term *frigging*). But these words gave way to *f——ing* at some later point. Most students of the patterns of word usage attribute the wide employment of the term to the experience of the Tommies, not that of the officers.

## Britain Rewards War Leaders

The services of General Douglas Haig, ultimately the supreme commander of all British forces in France, were evidently much appreciated by members of Parliament and others. That body made him an earl and voted to give him a kind of bonus, of 100,000 pounds, while through public subscription he was given Bemersyde Mansion. Admiral David Beatty, who by the end of the war commanded the Grand Fleet, was also made an earl and given 100,000 pounds by Parliament in 1919.

## Explosion at Verdun

On February 21, 1916, the German attack was opened by a bombardment more terrific than any the war had experienced to date. For no less than 12.5 hours large guns of every caliber poured 100,000 shells per hour on a front of only six miles. History had never seen such furious fire. It blotted out the French first lines, shattered the communication trenches, turned an entire forest into mounds of splinters, and altered the very shape of the hills. Messages had to be carried by groups of six soldiers with the hope that at least one would arrive at his destination. The lines of French and German forces wavered back and forth and hills changed hands several times in a struggle that did not grind to a bloody halt until October. The combined casualty count had passed the 900,000 mark; the battle was so demoralizing that the average soldier found the noxious gases from exploding shells a relief from the horrible odor of rotting human and horse flesh. Eventually France claimed the victory, achieving their rallying cry, "They shall not pass."

## Pressure of War on British Drinking Habits

Tampering with the availability, price, or quality of the workingmen's beer can threaten the life of a Cabinet. Yet, with the pressure of war and the need for increased and uninterrupted productivity, Prime Minister Lloyd George and Parliament violated all three of the taboos by the middle years of World War I. Drinking hours were cut down, creating a three-hour gap from 3:00 P.M. to 6:00 P.M., a practice that continued until 1987. On top of this, the strength of beer was reduced and its price increased. The government quickly realized that for many in the working class (both sexes) the war brought more work and greater income than they had ever experienced. Thus, one who enjoyed the pub might merely choose to work a half day or part of a week. In support of this approach to drink and the war effort, George V took a king's pledge of total abstention for the duration of the war. Few followed his lead, however, particularly neither of the wartime prime ministers, Asquith and Lloyd George.

## The Special Talents of Lawrence of Arabia

It is to the undeniable credit of the motion picture industry that many more people today have been introduced to at least the spectacular side of T. E. Lawrence than otherwise would have been. Lawrence was, at least for the Allies, the only old-style (i.e., Victorian) hero of the World War I. He was most persuasive and influential among Arab tribes and induced them to revolt against Turkish (German ally) rule. Yet it should be remembered that his chief tools were his solid academic background in archaeology and his gift for the Arabic language, not his study of public administration.

## The Inescapable Side Effects of War

Distinguished British historian A. J. P. Taylor has asserted that much of the impact of modern war on domestic society can be as subtle as it is extensive. For example, prior to 1914, the law-abiding Englishman could pass through life without any intrusion into his affairs by the state save for the post office and the policeman or constable. There was no passport required for entering or leaving the country (only Turkey and Russia required such papers in 1914); there were no limits on either monetary exchanges or tariffs on foreign goods; there was no required military service as there was on the Continent. Except for the items of education, health protection laws, a minor pension, and maximum working hours, the state did indeed leave the adult citizen to his or her own devices.

By the end of the war the state regulated dozens of crucial aspects of society, something that advanced further after World War II. Eventually England even resorted to universal conscription for all adult males, and deferment could only be gained by medical reasons or employment in an occupation essential to the war effort. This in turn brought into wide use a new term to the English vocabulary, *conscientious objector*, replacing the more common and colloquial *stackers*. There developed a system to regulate food production, distribution, and sale; all forms of transportation; rationing; and even the drinking hours at the pub. Street lights dimmed, news was censored, beer was watered, and even the clocks were changed.

An interesting aside to all of this was the role of Lord Rhondda, the wealthiest and most prominent mining and business magnate in South Wales. He was ultimately named Minister of Food and supervised all domestic supply and rationing, for which he was dubbed the "jam king" by British subjects, who still retained their sense of humor.

## Fiery Clemenceau: France's Last Card

When Georges Clemenceau became premier in November of 1917, France was a war-ravaged nation that had suffered millions of casualties, that had a serious problem of mutiny in the ranks, that was racked by defeatist propaganda at home, and that had witnessed the collapse of no less than five wartime ministries. No one had more political enemies in France than Clemenceau and the choice of him as premier said much about the grave condition of the French nation in spirit, personnel, and materiel. This fierce political warrior, however, had already fought for three generations, and was not like those who had plastered together governments characteristic of the Third Republic.

Already in his seventies, hunched over, sporting a snow-white walrus mustache, agnostic, anticlerical, a German-baiting nationalist, and the only member of the French legislature to have suffered the terms of the surrender to Germany back in 1871, he presented his plans to the Chamber of Deputies in what must have been one of the shortest speeches ever delivered to that body. He declared: "Home policy? I wage war! Foreign policy? I wage war! All the time I wage war." The German propagandist press observed the choice of this radical to head the war government and loudly asserted that France had played her "last card." Later, after the Allied victory, a French journalist retrieved that piece of defeatism, reprinted the enemy's claims, and then simply agreed with the assertion, adding, "Yes, and it was trump."

# Battle of Caporetto

During World War I the Italians had suffered through so many battles along the Isonzo River front that Caporetto is sometimes called the "twelfth Isonzo." Austro-German forces struck with such swift force in late October of 1917 that by November 4 Italian forces were hurled back across the Piave River, their losses exceeding 300,000, and it appeared that the invading troops would overrun Venice.

What makes this bloody disaster of particular interest is the fact that a young, American volunteer ambulance driver of lieutenant rank in the Italian army, already once wounded, observed the resulting bloody chaos, desertions, and accompanying psychological collapse. He was Ernest Hemingway, and it is not without logic that a similar, but fictional, American in the same role witnessed the same horrors in *A Farewell to Arms*. That character fled to Stresa, joined his beloved English nurse, crossed to Swiss sanctuary by rowboat, and also said "a farewell to arms."

# Lloyd George's Opinions
# of Fellow War Leaders

By the time David Lloyd George became British prime minister (he also remained minister of war) in 1916 he had logged two decades of tough battles in domestic politics as leader of the radical wing of the Liberal Party. He had a reputation as a smooth, cunning, and crafty politician in public life and a somewhat rakish philanderer in private life. Two of the world leaders who joined him at the Versailles Peace Conference in 1919 offered broad contrast. The U.S. president, Woodrow Wilson, had established an idealistic position, evangelical in tone, and even used biblical language to speak about peace arrangements (the Fourteen Points, the "Covenant"). On the other hand, the French premier, Georges Clemenceau, with his record of baiting both Germans and Roman Catholic clergy, acted like a man determined to live up to his nickname, "the Tiger."

Thus there were times when Lloyd George expressed a somewhat cynical view of his role as one of the so-called Big Three. For pictures he found himself seated between the evangelical from across the Atlantic, who had been called the "Princeton prophet," and the agnostic firebrand, whose first reaction to Wilson's Fourteen Points was, "God Almighty only had ten." Recalling that unenviable position, the British prime minister said, "There I was, God on one side, the devil on the other."

# Clemenceau's View
# of the Prospects for Peace

At the conclusion of debates over the Versailles Treaty, which ended World War I, at a time when many spoke of the recently concluded struggle as the "war to end all wars," French Premier Georges Clemenceau, before the Chamber of Deputies, was most circumspect with his words. "What you are about to vote on today," he told the Chamber, "is not even a beginning, but a beginning of a beginning." He conceded that one of the right-wing deputies had been correct when in despair he said, "Your treaty condemns France to eternal vigilance." That, said the Tiger, was exactly the case, since "peace is only war pursued by other means." Like Winston Churchill a generation later, Clemenceau was offering his countrymen blood, toil, tears, and sweat at a time when they desperately wanted rest and relief.

Three years later in 1922, as Clemenceau rested in embittered retirement, he told a young admirer: "Everything I have done has been wasted. In twenty years, France will be dead." Twenty years after that statement was made half of France was occupied by German troops and the other half was administered by Vichy collaborationists. Maybe the words of Raymond Couly in 1936 held the answer—"When a country hasn't an army that fits its politics, it must have policies that fit its army."

## Surprise at Discovering Yanks without Hatred

Erich Maria Remarque, who left the University of Münster to fight as a German soldier in the trenches of World War I, in 1929 published a worldwide best-seller called *All Quiet on the Western Front*. While his book presented a vivid picture of the horrors of war to a large audience, he chose to go further with his story in *The Road Back*, which he published in 1931. In this book he discussed postwar disillusionment and the problems of adjustment to civilian life in an economically ravaged society. Among his many experiences, one in particular stands out for the American reader. Remarque and other infantrymen, undernourished and with torn or rotting uniforms, were subjected to a long walk home through northwestern France and their homeland across the Rhine. Fatigue added to their slow progress, and they were quickly overtaken by American soldiers also moving toward Germany. Remarque became seriously confused by the conduct of these troops from across the Atlantic—troops who all appeared young and well fed, had fresh uniforms, and had friendly if not jovial dispositions. They even shared some of their food with the tired and hungry "enemy."

It took a while before Remarque was able to sort out the reasons for their behavior, but after much thought he figured it out. The

Yanks were not next-door neighbors to any of the European nations, and had no historical memories of armies locked in combat. They had not suffered under fire for four long years in the trenches of the western front. They had no inbred hatreds that produced immediate animosity toward defeated Germans. There were simply no reasons for an American soldier from the upper Missouri Valley to automatically dislike Germans. What Remarque, once back home, did not see was the irritation among Frenchmen when Americans failed to display a sufficiently vengeful spirit.

## The Sinister Sicilian Mafia

A Sicilian, upon seeing a prancing stallion, well caparisoned, with arched neck, dilated nostrils, and fiery eyes, might easily exclaim, "What a mafioso horse!" This observation is made by Luigi Barzini in his book *The Italians*. The reference obviously is not related to a secret society that has, since the nineteenth century, permeated large sections of Sicilian and eventually all of Italian society. In Sicily the Mafia has been a real and significant fact of life. Most citizens of the northern Sicilian areas pay tribute to some sort of local boss of some position or station in the community. All accept this truism of Sicilian life (until 1988 at least). But the relationship between the Mafia and a victim thereof is not limited to the mere collection of money. Sooner or later the victim will be asked to perform a favor in return for services rendered. Such a request must not be refused. All conform, of course, because they want to avoid trouble. The question is, trouble with whom?

At the close of World War I the Italian premier, Vittorio Orlando, who sat as one of the Big Four with Woodrow Wilson, David Lloyd George, and Georges Clemenceau at the first round of peace negotiations at Versailles, was a Sicilian who was a renowned specialist in his nation's constitutional law. He had originally stood for election in his local Sicilian district, which he had to win in order to play the big game in Rome—the game of *combinazione* that infected the Italian legislature like a burgeoning tumor. Years later, in 1946, in the first free election since Mussolini, a large canvas sign could be seen displayed grandly in the town of Partinico, near Palermo. Orlando had been elected there for the first time in 1897. The canvas read, "Vote for Vittorio Emanuele Orlando, l'amico delgi amici [the friend of friends]." Now, let us guess who the "friends" were (are) and the degree of clarity with which each voter comprehended the glaring message.

The best scholarship on the famous secret society provides an explanation for the term *Mafia*—it is an acronym of the words *Mazzini Autorizza Furti Incendi Avvelenamenti*. The translation is, "Mazzini authorizes theft, arson, poisoning."

## British Lifestyle during the Interwar Years

On September 10, 1931, Lord Robert Cecil, speaking for the British government, told the League of Nations Assembly, "There has scarcely been a period in the world's history when war seems less likely than it does at present." Just a week after those remarks were made, Japanese troops moved into Manchuria.

The motorcar had a great formative influence on western European life in the post–World War I era. There were fewer than 200,000 registered private cars on British roads in 1920, but by 1939 the number was nearer the 2 million level. Despite this, until 1934 one had only to be age 17 and claim physical fitness to operate an auto. Only after that year did newcomers need to pass a test. The speed limit of 30 miles per hour applied only in urban areas with street lights, and no special motor police were created. Thus, there were more people killed on the roads in 1934 than in 1964, when the number of cars had increased to 12 million.

There was no appliance more widely used in the British home during the interwar period than the wireless set (radio). Its use was so dominant that attendance declined at social centers, churches, clubs, and literary societies. Even beer consumption did not pick up with the increase of prosperity as the 1930s wore on. Because beer drinking is a social activity and associated with the pub, those who stayed at home with the wireless chose tea. Even factories favored the tea break instead of a midday visit to the pub, which caused drunkenness convictions to decline by half during the 1930s.

Outside the home, the cinema defeated all public entertainment competitors, despite the expanding popularity of association football, sports betting, and greyhound racing. The advent of cinema as a recreational pleasure contributed to the certain death of traveling drama companies, the music hall, and regional theaters. Cinemas operated seven evenings per week, offered the escape of fantasyland, and had programs for every age group. In the 1930s, a new and super expansion of the cinema occurred when *The Jazz Singer* led the way for the "talkies." In England, this new form spelled domination of the screen by products from a foreign land, the United States. Only Britain's Alfred Hitchcock emerged to world renown during these years. One of the ironies of cinema popularity was an attempt to thwart Sunday performances by enforcing the Sunday Observance Act of 1782, which brought sufficient outcry to have the issue given over to local poll, thereby ending the problem.

## Hitler: A Memorable Man

Imagine a scene in a Vienna apartment, in about 1919, where about a dozen young people of university age have gathered. Perhaps there is a gramophone playing background music. Most people have a wine glass in hand and are engaged in light conversation, but one guest sits alone on the couch, where he has been for some time in morose silence. Then, among the various conversations someone says the word *Jew*. At this point the silent young man (Hitler) jumps to his feet and unleashes a 20-minute sarcastic and hateful tirade against the Jews, sprinkling his speech with analytical details. At the sermon's end he immediately sits down and again becomes silent. Most of those present at this gathering will likely remember both the young man and the incident.

A few years after this occasion, Hitler attributed special value to what he considered a typical Jewish tactic—the "big lie"—and then proceeded to recommend its use in *Mein Kampf*. He assured readers that the big lie always carried a certain force of credibility, since the simple masses react emotionally with their somewhat primitive minds. Also, because the masses often tell small lies in little matters, but would be ashamed to resort to large-scale falsehoods, they would never believe that others could have the impudence to significantly distort the truth. Years later both Hitler and Propaganda Minister Joseph Goebbels would turn this postulate into a cornerstone of Nazi propagandistic journalism.

Another aspect of Hitler's speech-making style has been carefully documented by British historian Alan Bullock, who points to the leader's slow, hammering method of public speaking and his use of verbs easily visualized by a mass audience (mash, bash, smash, crush).

Of all of Hitler's speeches, none ever measured up to the power and invective carried by the *Sportspalast* oration on September 28th, 1938. In that address, to which Hitler personally invited the British ambassador Sir Horace Wilson, he declared that the Czech state began as a lie, saying, "There is no such thing as a Czechoslovak nation, but only Czechs and Slovaks, and the Slovaks do not wish to have anything to do with the Czechs."

## Hitler Ruins the Word Aryan for Future Use

Until the late nineteenth-century racial writings of Arthur Gobineau and Houston Stewart Chamberlain, and more particularly the writings and verbal rantings of Hitler and his propaganda machine, the term *Aryan* was an acceptable and most useful tool for historians and anthropologists. Specifically, it was and is a term that connotes language groupings and the very people who, centuries before Jesus, moved from northern Europe to establish societies bordering the Mediterranean Sea (Dorians, Ionians, Etruscans). The term *Semitic* has been properly employed in the same fashion, designating the peoples of a language grouping geographically located in the Near East and the northern reaches of Africa. This usage places Jews and most Arabic people in the same linguistic cast as classified culturally. Then came Hitler, *Mein Kampf*, and the scurrilous writings associated with the Third Reich, which employed the term *Aryan* strictly as a racial definition that referred specifically to peoples of Nordic-Teutonic ethnic heritage. According to this position, Aryans have blond hair, blue eyes, and sturdy northern European features and bloodlines. Thus, by the close of World War II, most scholars were forced to use the term *Indo-European* instead of *Aryan* to convey the same meaning, lest they be misunderstood or accused of employing racial terminology.

## *Historical Value of the Film* Cabaret

Christopher William Bradshaw-Isherwood (b. 1904) had for some time been a critically acclaimed writer without popular success when he moved from his native Britain to work as a private tutor and free-lance journalist in Berlin between 1929 and 1933. The themes he later developed from that experience finally brought him fame as a writer. The reputation he established by the late 1930s inspired the play *I Am a Camera* (based on the *Isherwood Papers*) in 1951 (film, 1955) and the musical *Cabaret* (1966), which as a 1972 film won world acclaim and many awards.

The author was in Berlin during the very years that witnessed the conspicuous decay of the shaky Weimar Republic and the final rise to power of Hitler and the Nazi regime. The award-winning film offers much more than mere entertainment; when Joel Grey sings "Money, Money" and the camera pans the audience, the brown uniforms with swastika armbands are not there just to add color.

## *Race and the Berlin Olympics*

By the time of the 1936 Olympic Games Hitler and the Nazi party had already been in power three years, and for more than a decade Hitler's masterwork of political ideology, *Mein Kampf*, had been in print. Millions purchased the book after 1933 as a sort of personal insurance policy, to conspicuously show their "support" for the Nazis. Along with his belief in the superiority of the Aryan race and his vicious attacks on Jews, Hitler warned of the dangers of "mongrelizing" a pure race with the likes of African blacks or Negroid blood of any kind. Lest one believe the dictator had had no previous contact with blacks, it must be remembered that he had served on the western front during World War I, where the French employed colonial regiments from Africa.

Ironically, Berlin hosted the Summer Olympics in 1936, and many of the events were personally attended by the Führer. Although Germany proved a winner in total points, and Hitler wished the event to be an international demonstration of the superiority of the Aryan race, the most popular events were not won by Germans. A black American, Jesse Owens, won the 100- and 200-meter sprints, while another black American, Archie Williams, won the 400-meter race. Owens also posted a first in the long jump and both Owens and Williams were members of the victorious 400-meter relay team.

## Hitler: A Brute Who Admired Brutes

Napoleon Bonaparte, after eight years of diplomatic dealings with Russia, implied that when Europeans were considered as a whole it was evident that the Russians were something apart. According to Napoleon, "Scratch a Russian, find a Tartar." Hitler made a similar statement in reference to the Soviet leader Joseph Stalin before the outbreak of World War II. After assessing the European diplomatic scene, Hitler asserted that there were only three "real" statesmen left in all of Europe: "Myself, Il Duce [Mussolini], and Genghis Khan." Hitler then went on to surprise the rest of Europe, including Mussolini, by signing a special pact with Stalin that proved but a prelude to the invasion and dismemberment of Poland by the two powers.

## How Appeasement Became a Dirty Word

As a result of pressure mounted by Hitler's Nazi Germany and by the three million Germans residing in the Sudeten portion of Czechoslovakia during the summer of 1938, the two nations appeared headed for armed conflict by September. Two mediation visits by British Prime Minister Neville Chamberlain with Hitler in Germany had not produced a solution; the dictator had in fact expanded his demands regarding the Sudetenland after each visit. France, a guarantor (along with Russia) of Czech sovereignty and territorial integrity, mobilized part of her armed forces in response to German moves.

Finally, Hitler agreed to a conference, apparently persuaded by his Rome-Berlin Axis ally Mussolini, to whom both President

Franklin Roosevelt and Prime Minister Chamberlain had appealed for a pacifying influence. Hitler, German Foreign Minister Ribbentrop, Mussolini, Italian Foreign Minister Ciano, Chamberlain, and French Premier Daladier conferred in a lengthy September 29 session that lasted until midnight and produced an agreement without the presence of either Czech or Russian representatives. While Germany gained considerable Czech territory and 3.5 million inhabitants, within a month Czech territory was surrendered to both Hungary and Poland, and the remaining area disintegrated into semi-autonomous Czech, Slovak, and Ruthenian units.

The ultimate result had serious implications for democratic nations, since it could be argued successfully, as Winston Churchill had charged for some years, that the settlement was a blatant desertion by a democratic nation (France) that had pledged, either by treaty or other arrangement, to defend democratic institutions. The term *appeasement* quickly became the catchword in the press and in political parlance on both sides of the Atlantic for any weak or conciliatory response to the demands or actions of dictators. It rapidly became a word with negative connotations and has retained much of the same flavor to this day. Though the crowd cheered when Chamberlain met the press at the airport upon his return from the Munich Conference and, waving a copy of the agreement, said, "I believe it is peace in our time," few felt such confidence a week later. Indeed, Premier Daladier was surprised by the cheers in Paris, for he felt the full meaning of the shameful arrangement to which he had contributed.

When Chamberlain appeared before cameras during the departures and returns of his three German trips, he was conspicuously dressed as an English gentleman, with an umbrella hanging from one arm. That umbrella soon became a symbol of appeasement. During the Cuban missile crisis faced by John Kennedy in the first year of his presidency (1961), the symbol reappeared in the press. When it was still undetermined how strong a stand President Kennedy might take on the presence of Soviet missiles in Cuba, a Maulden cartoon without caption appeared in the press. It portrayed Kennedy, in the clothing of a cowboy, on horseback in a desert scene (New Frontier). He wore a gun belt with two holsters, and an umbrella was conspicuously fitted in each.

# An Outsider's View
# of France's Third Republic

As Hitler's *Wehrmacht* closed in on Paris during the second week of June in 1940, the last of the Third Republic's premiers worked in feverish exhaustion at the Chateau de Chissay near Bordeaux. He was faced with deciding whether to continue French resistance from North Africa and on the seas or instead seek as early as possible the best negotiable terms of armistice and surrender. That tragic figure was Paul Reynaud. Defeatism stalked his every move as cabinet members and top generals moved to the latter choice. The best foreign observer's account of those days has been furnished by General Edward Spears, Churchill's liaison officer, who was fluently bilingual.

Spears described the situation when he arrived at the chateau on June 13 as "a mad-house." To his astonishment, in the court-yard he "saw . . . Madame de Portes (Reynaud's mistress) in a dressing-gown over red pajamas, directing traffic from the steps." There was a muddle of "indescribable confusion" at the heart of what was supposed to be the brain center of France. The general's few meetings with the premier were regularly interrupted by Helen de Portes, causing Spears to concede that he had reached the limit of his endurance for her, and he went on to describe her: "She is ugly, *mal soignée*, dirty, nasty, and half-demented, and a sore trial for me." The truth is that she exercised more influence on Reynaud than was good for France, to the chagrin of Churchill and DeGaulle (who was in London). This episode and others caused General Spears to later make reference to the slime that passes for government in France, a remark that reached French ears.

There have been volumes written to demonstrate France's lack of preparedness in September of 1939, and how little had been done by the next spring to correct the problem. A telling example of this unfortunate situation is the account supplied by French novelist, biographer, and literary critic André Maurois, who was called to serve as a captain and liaison officer to Belgian authorities. Maurois soon received a written order that all officers were to arm themselves with a proper pistol of military issue. He went to the supply sergeant and tendered his request for a pistol, displaying the order. He was told that supply was clean out of pistols, and had been for some time, upon which he asked when some would be available. The response was that orders had been placed for the weapons in Italy and arrival time was unknown. This was quite strange, since Italy was part of the Rome-Tokyo-Berlin Axis, and would attack France a few months later.

## Mussolini's Hasty Move to War Had a Heavy Price

By the beginning of World War II in September of 1939, Italy was already joined in alliance with Hitler's Germany in what was known as the Rome-Tokyo-Berlin Axis. In April of 1940 Hitler's forces occupied Denmark and invaded Norway, then continued the thrust into the Netherlands, Belgium, and Luxembourg in May. Following the collapse of Belgian resistance the German armored divisions turned south. It was at that very point that Il Duce, Benito Mussolini, was forced to make what proved to be the most momentous decision of his prematurely shortened life.

Some factors he faced in making that decision and its unfortunate results deserve special comment. The diaries of his son-in-law and foreign minister, Count Ciano, reveal much about that crucial time:

1. Mussolini was a very nervous man during the two years prior to 1939, because every time he met with Hitler the German dictator unloaded his vituperations about smashing this or that nation, and Il Duce knew that the Nazis had the materials and resources to do what the Führer desired.

   Italy was aboard the German ship but did not have sufficient resources to defend itself, and no aid or supplies had yet been offered by the Germans. Il Duce's peninsula nation was exposed to both British and French sea or air power, and entry into the fray on the side of Hitler might cause situations that Italy was not prepared for.

2. On the other hand, continued neutrality seemed out of the question, for how could Hitler permit the entire southern part of

Europe to remain open or exposed? Obviously, Hitler would take
the attitude that Italy was either with him or against him, and if it
were the latter Italy might very well be occupied like France.

3.  By the late spring of 1940 it appeared that all resistance was being
    successfully defeated by the German thrust. If Mussolini wished
    to be second in command among the states that would compose
    Hitler's new Fortress Europe he would need to share in the
    victory.

4.  Other nations, sensing the Italian dilemma, urged Mussolini to
    remain neutral. A personal plea came from U.S. President Franklin
    Roosevelt. Just three days before the German *Wehrmacht* marched
    into Paris, Il Duce made the fatal plunge, or, as Roosevelt said, the
    "one who held the dagger has struck it into the back of its
    neighbor."

With this background, we can move on to one of the more
humorous developments of World War II. As the sequence of
events unfolded from late 1939 onward, Mussolini had created
problems for Hitler by moving on Albania and then on Greece in
1940. However, not only did the Greeks halt and then push the
Italian troops out of Greece, but, by the time of the Italian invasion
of France (June 10), they were in the process of removing them
from Albania as well.

Intelligence reports of these developments reached the French
troops that, although outnumbered by three to one, had pinned
down the Italian divisions a few kilometers within French
borders, causing a stalemate. Upon hearing the news of developments in Albania, these French troops used the cover of darkness
to move out into the no man's land between the two battle lines,
and there posted signs facing the Italian lines. At daybreak Italian
officers who pointed their field glasses toward French lines were
greeted by large signs that had messages written in Italian. The
signs read, "Attention Greeks, please stop here, you are now
entering France."

Humor quite aside, the result of the Italian military failure
forced Hitler and the German forces to act to save face in the
Balkan region, which would become a critical factor in the future
struggle with Russia. Occupation of that southern European area
proved to be a heavy drain on German resources, just as it had
been for Napoleon's 200,000 troops who were tied down in Spain

when he marched on Moscow, to say nothing of the later Axis prerequisite of defending Italy proper after 1942.

## Fascist Politicians Play Hardball

Italian fascists were brutal toward political opponents both during their rise to prominence and while solidifying their position. One of their tactics proved quite effective in the game of physical intimidation while leaving no visible marks on the victim's body. Mussolini's loyal cadres would merely kidnap an opposition leader, take him to a distant and isolated spot, force him to drink an entire liter of castor oil, and then leave him to fend for himself. The results were essentially similar to those that brought death to Saint Louis in North Africa during his second crusade.

## Montgomery's Counterattack at El Alamein

Despite successes at Tobruk, Benghasi, and other Italian North African strongholds in 1941, the following year found British forces pushed from Libya into Egypt and fighting to hold the lines just 70 miles west of the city of Alexandria. The reason for the reversal lay mainly with strong Axis reinforcements from Germany, who were specifically trained and equipped for desert warfare and brilliantly commanded by General Erwin Rommel. The British move to halt the Axis advance is known as the Battle of Alamein and it made General Bernard Montgomery a war hero. A particularly interesting feature of this episode is the intelligence report that led to the British commander's decision to counterattack at Alamein.

As recounted by Edgar "Bill" Williams, who had participated in preparing the report, from his position as Warden of Rhodes House at Oxford University, it was determined that the large portion of the enemy forces were in fact Italian and were merely "corseted" by a much smaller number of Germans. This information, combined with the knowledge of previous British success against Italian forces, produced the decision to move against Rommel.

# Teaching about the Era of World War II

Teachers of world or European history obviously have a broad selection of material with which to relate the character of World War II, but direct comparisons to students' lives often help them truly understand the nature of everyday life during this period. To students who turned 16 in the spring of 1988, the distance between Louis XIV and Charles de Gaulle probably seems rather short. Their fathers did not leave home when the students were six, not returning until they were ten, nor did their fathers speak of exotic places with names like Java, Iwo Jima, Normandy, or Ramagen.

Furthermore, such students may find it hard to comprehend the strange and, to many, oppressive term *rationing*. Yet, there are men 65 years of age and older all over Europe and the U.S. who have proudly stated, "I fought in the Big One." Here are some miscellaneous facts that may help students better understand "the Big One":

The years between 1941 and 1945 saw the U.S. replace Sweden as the largest per capita consumer of coffee. Anyone who understands the demands of World War II would not require the services of a sociologist to explain that development.

Though most nations had before suffered the stresses of shortages and rationing, it was a first for Americans. One of the products of that experience was a popular song that ran, "Yes, we have no bananas, we have no bananas today." There were also shortages of meat, chocolate, silk stockings, and sugar.

The prime minister of Britain, Winston Churchill, when addressing members of the House of Commons amid the rubble that Hitler's *Luftwaffe* had made of the Parliament buildings, appeared in proper gentleman's dress, but his clothing was rather conspicuously patched.

A strategist who comprehended the importance of production and supply in modern warfare would readily have predicted the victory of the Allied powers over the Axis powers as early as 1942. Such a prediction would have been predicated on the fact that oil had become the crucial commodity in modern warfare by that time and the United States and its allies controlled the output of 86 percent of the world's oil supply. The Allies entered 1942 with a 60–40 percentage edge over the Axis powers in manufactured goods, and had soon solved the rubber problem by rapid development of synthetics. Certain confinement of the extent of Axis control put time on the Allied side.

Transportation was also a crucial factor, since U.S. products had to be moved across either one or the other of the major oceans. Surface sea transportation became a game of hide-and-seek that depended on technological means of detection and defense. This lesson hit hard when several U.S. ships were carrying tank parts for assembly in North Africa. All the engines were unwisely put on one ship, and that ship was sunk. Of course, this led to the special significance of that "electric eye" known as radar and the later perfection of sonar. By 1943 the Atlantic became a bridge of boats.

By 1944 the commodities being shipped to U.S. allies had expanded to such a wide variety that the list included everything from Nucoa margarine to Camel cigarettes. The Soviets ingeniously removed cigarette packages from the cartons before distribution and placed a strip over the top of each that read, "Compliments of the Communist Party, New York City."

The early and great victories of the Japanese had lifted the reputation of the Japanese soldiers to unexampled heights. In much of the Orient this reputation eclipsed the idea of any Western superiority, and Japanese soldiers by 1941 often sang the following song as they marched into battle:

> Across the sea
> Corpses in the water;
> Across the mountain,
> Corpses heaped upon the field;
> I shall die only for the Emperor,
> I shall never look back.

The turning point in that spirit and in military reality came with a single crucial naval clash at Midway in June of 1942, when a technically smaller U.S. fleet defeated the Japanese Imperial Fleet and turned it back, removing forever from the Japanese navy the initiative and the ability to control the course of the war in the Pacific. U.S. resources, productivity, and economic mobilization doomed the Japanese to a holding pattern: defeat was only a matter of time.

Many millions of words have been written and spoken on the subject of the U.S. decision to use the atom bomb against the Japanese. This author heard a university professor as late as 1968 charge that the essential motivation of the U.S. was clearly racial, since the bomb was not used against Germany. Of course, that is a moot point because the bomb was not prepared for use when Germany collapsed in the spring of 1945. However, there are some undeniably salient facts that must be considered when this issue arises. First, it seemed apparent that the Japanese, who had proven to be zealous if not fanatical soldiers, intended to defend the numerous islands that constitute the archipelago of Japan to the last man or woman. Second, before the bomb's availability was certain there had been prepared Operations Olympic and Coronet, comprising the combined forces of the U.S., Britain, France, the Netherlands, New Zealand, and Australia. Both operations poised the forces for air and amphibious invasion and conquest of the islands. It was estimated that such an invasion would leave millions of Japanese military and civilian dead or wounded; several hundred thousand was the conservative estimate of Allied losses. Third, the raids on Hiroshima and Nagasaki produced less than 200,000 in dead and wounded, much fewer than would have been produced if the atom bombs had not been used. Japan was not defeated militarily nor stripped of the means to fight on, but the nation's will to go on had been broken, just as it had for Germany in the fall of 1918.

# The Effects of Wartime Rationing on Civilians

Despite the general prosperity enjoyed by Americans as opposed to much of the world's population during World War II, many materials and commodities were in short supply. Many basic food products, gasoline, tires, and other items crucial to the war effort could be purchased only with ration stamps that were of limited supply. The last domestic autos produced in the U.S. were the 1942 models that had already been completed by the time of the attack on Pearl Harbor in December of 1941, and most of those were driven by retail auto dealers and doctors. Owing to the shortage of silk (prior to the wide use of nylon), women stood in long lines on the occasional instances when hose became available.

Most of this, of course, directly affected adults rather than children and teenagers, who were affected more conspicuously by other shortages. Many brands of candy and candy bars disappeared for nearly four years, among them Three Musketeers, Milky Way, and Butterfinger, while both Juicyfruit and Doublemint gums were not to be found on the home front. Bubblegum suffered the same fate, and when it reappeared again in late 1945, purchase was limited until the supply caught up with demand. There were even long periods when ice cream was unavailable and soda fountains could offer only orange or orange-pineapple sherbet that was artificially flavored. Many people who were born during the war years have never realized that many of their favorite treats were not new products (for example, Baby Ruth), but simply had been distributed almost exclusively among military personnel in the war years. Chocolate bars served as currency in many foreign and all occupied countries during the war.

## Preview of the Cold War: Truman and Stalin at Potsdam

U.S. President Harry S Truman will forever be referred to in world history as the leader at the forefront of such developments as the Marshall Plan for European recovery, the preliminary foundations of the NATO Alliance to resist Soviet aggression toward western Europe, and a doctrine to aid Turkey, Greece, and other nations in preventing the overthrow of their legitimate governments by domestic Communist partisans who were armed and supported by Soviet aid. Little was subtle about Truman's policies, for he was a plain and frank-speaking man who saw the problems of freedom, fear, war, and hunger in very practical terms: the first of the four was to be protected and encouraged, the last three thwarted.

Truman had not been party to the planning conferences of the Big Three (Roosevelt, Churchill, and Stalin) and their lieutenants during World War II, and in terms of agreements or concessions made was an uninformed vice-president. The death of Roosevelt in the spring of 1945 thrust Truman into a role as one of the Big Three and brought him face to face with Stalin and Churchill in decisions regarding the terms of German surrender, reparations, occupation zones, and the re-establishment of postwar governments. What follows are this author's recollections of a national television news forum in the early 1960s. This forum provided information on the course of events at Potsdam and the shaping of some of Truman's attitudes toward Soviet leader Stalin. The chief guest was Robert Murphy, personal aide to the U.S. president who accompanied him at both conference table and dinner table.

Murphy explained that in the days prior to his arrival at the old palace of Prussian King Frederick the Great, Truman had received briefings from experts of various kinds. One had convinced the president that one of the best ways to alleviate hunger and restore economic security to Europe was to place all major continental waterways under international supervision, thereby guaranteeing the free and essential distribution of goods to all areas. Thus, at an appropriate time in the discussions, Truman proposed the internationalization of major waterways to encourage widespread distribution of services and supplies to heal the wounds of a war-torn Europe and relieve hunger while economic systems were being rebuilt. Before there was even any discussion of the idea Stalin responded firmly, "Nyet." Truman turned toward Murphy, and under his breath said, "Why, the dirty son of a bitch." Truman then assumed an educator's role, indicating that maybe the Soviet leader had not fully understood either the intent or importance of the proposal, and restated the suggestion in more detail. The result was abrupt and even more forceful: "Nyet." Again Truman said to Murphy, "Why, the dirty son of a bitch." As the session was finally adjourned, the question arose of what exact statement was to be released to the press regarding any progress or developments during the day. Truman proposed that the press release indicate the proposal he had made on behalf of the United States, which brought a loud and emphatic "No"—in English—from Stalin. Truman once more remarked, "Why, the dirty son of a bitch."

During the conference the three statesmen alternated in hosting the others and their staff for dinner. When Truman hosted the first time, Stalin grasped the arm of a presidential staff member when he attempted to pour wine in the Soviet's glass. Stalin pulled back the towel in which the bottle was wrapped, observed the domestic American label, and blurted out, "Nyet." Truman made his usual remark to Murphy, and the phrase soon came to embody Truman's evaluation of the Soviet leader and his policies in the cold war years to come.

# *Quotes from Churchill*

It is rare for an individual so involved in domestic and international politics as Winston Churchill to establish a world-renowned reputation for literature (Nobel Prize), historical writing, and painting. Of course, his oratorical skills were also quite well known. The following are a few of this author's favorite Churchill quotes:

> When someone close to Labour Party leader Clement Atlee, who was Churchill's political opponent, remarked, "Mr. Atlee is a very modest man," Churchill immediately responded, "Mr. Atlee has much about which to be modest." Churchill was later heard to say, "An empty cab pulled up, and Mr. Atlee got out."

> By the end of World War II Churchill's face was as familiar worldwide as the voice of Bing Crosby. While he was campaigning for re-election in his district, a female admirer shook his hand and declared that her baby looked just like the prime minister. Churchill responded, "Madame, all babies look like me."

> Tradition has it that Lady Astor once told Churchill in a fit of anger that if she were married to him she would put poison in his tea, to which he answered, "And if I were married to you I would drink it."

> To a woman with whom he had exchanged some hostile words, Churchill finally said, "Madame, you are ugly," to which she retorted, "and you Mr. Churchill are drunk." Churchill added, "But in the morning, I will be sober."

# General Reference Works

*The Cambridge Ancient History.* 12 vols. New York: Macmillan, 1928–1939.

*The Cambridge Medieval History.* 8 vols. Cambridge: Cambridge University Press, 1964–1967.

*The Cambridge Modern History.* 13 vols. Cambridge: Cambridge University Press, 1902–1912.

These three multivolume works present both a general and detailed study of the fundamental origins and development of what we loosely call Western civilization. Each set, completed under general editorship, is available at college or university libraries and at many public libraries as well. As a group they represent the best and most balanced sources of basic, factual information for a survey history from ancient Near Eastern times well into the twentieth century.

Durant, Will and Ariel. *The Story of Civilization.* 11 vols. New York: Simon and Schuster, 1954–1975.

The Durants' 11-volume study commences with our ancient Oriental heritage and ends with the career of the great general Napoleon and the impact of the Napoleonic Age. Some have said it represents not an even survey, but rather what Will and Ariel Durant have found most interesting about Western civilization. There is some truth to that, and this is one of the best general resources for anecdotal material about important events. It also leans heavily on the humanistic and cultural developments of history. Brief biographical sketches are provided for all historical figures who receive substantial attention in the work. This is a rich source of quotations and snippets from literature and other printed works. All of the chapters are heavily footnoted, and each volume has a lengthy bibliography mostly composed of primary source materials.

Florinsky, Michael T. *Russia: A History and an Interpretation.* 2 vols. New York: Macmillan, 1953.

More than a mere reporting of events in basic chronological sequence, the two Florinsky volumes represent a detailed survey of Russian imperial history with an emphasis on the period since Peter the Great (1689–1725). The author deals in healthy fashion with cultural movements and offers special analysis of key literary developments and those persons who contributed to the evolution of the Russian language.

Holborn, Hajo. *A History of Modern Germany.* 3 vols. New York: A. A. Knopf, 1959–1969.

For several years this work has been the standard general compilation of German history from late Roman times to the mid-twentieth century. In just three volumes Holborn has included extensive treatments and evaluations of various evolutionary movements (for example, Romanticism), generous quotations, and relevant and interesting biographical details. Teachers will find these volumes most useful for German history since the Treaty of Utrecht in 1713.

*The Oxford History of England.* 15 vols. Oxford: Clarendon Press and Oxford University Press, 1937–1965.

This master collection, originally produced under the general editorship of Geoffrey Barraclough, remains the most complete single survey of English history. The first volume is confined to Britain under Roman rule, while the last volume closes with the end of World War II. Chapters concentrate on particular themes such as politics, religion, literature and the arts, and (in modern times) foreign policy. Footnotes include brief biographical sketches of all important individuals, and the appendix of each volume provides a wealth of reference materials. Only the last volume, *England 1914–1945*, has been published in paperback.

Taylor, A. J. P. *The Hapsburg Monarchy, 1809–1918*. London: H. Hamilton, 1948.

A. J. P. Taylor is also the author of the last volume of the Oxford collection discussed above. He writes well, with wit, and has an excellent command of the Slavic nuances so essential to the study of eastern Europe. Both this and the aforementioned Oxford volume were used extensively for the nineteenth-century discussion and British topics for the period 1914–1945.

Wright, Gordon. *France in Modern Times*. Chicago: Rand McNally College Publishing, 1974.

Gordon Wright has served as a distinguished professor at Stanford University and also as U.S. Minister for Cultural Affairs to the Fifth French Republic. He, too, provides a special wit and insights into the character of key personalities, and writes very readable history. This work is probably the most commonly used single-volume history of France in advanced-level college courses, and each section includes an annotated bibliography.

# Index